REBEL CHEF

ALSO BY DOMINIQUE CRENN

Atelier Crenn:
Metamorphosis of Taste

REBEL CHEF

IN SEARCH OF WHAT MATTERS

——

DOMINIQUE CRENN

with Emma Brockes

PENGUIN PRESS | NEW YORK | 2020

PENGUIN PRESS
An imprint of Penguin Random House LLC
penguinrandomhouse.com

All photographs, unless credited below, are courtesy of the author.
Pages 88, 133, 167, 176, 178, 196, 200, 203, 217: By Jordan Wise
Page 156: Courtesy of the Food Network
Pages 170, 194: By Marc Fiorito
Page 227: By Kimberly Zerkel

Library of Congress Cataloging-in-Publication Data

Names: Crenn, Dominique, author. | Brockes, Emma, author.
Title: Rebel chef : in search of what matters / Dominique Crenn with Emma Brockes.
Description: New York : Penguin Press, 2020. |
Identifiers: LCCN 2020001774 (print) | LCCN 2020001775 (ebook) |
ISBN 9780735224742 (hardcover) | ISBN 9780735224759 (ebook)
Subjects: LCSH: Crenn, Dominique. | Cooks—United States—Biography.
Classification: LCC TX649.C74 A3 2020 (print) | LCC TX649.C74 (ebook) |
DDC 641.5092 [B]—dc23
LC record available at https://lccn.loc.gov/2020001774
LC ebook record available at https://lccn.loc.gov/2020001775

Printed in the United States of America
3   5   7   9   10   8   6   4   2

Designed by Amanda Dewey

To Maria, l'amour de ma vie.
Un sourire, a laugh
Un regard, your eyes
Une pensée, my heart
Un baiser, your lips
Un rêve, you and I

CONTENTS

——

Part Three

REBEL CHEF

PROLOGUE

When I was six months old, I was left in the care of an orphanage near Paris and it was from here, a few months later, that my parents adopted me. As a child, I loved to hear the story of how they chose me that day; of how my brother, whom they had adopted months earlier, came over and spontaneously gave me a hug. Much later, in adulthood, I would learn something of the unhappy life of my birth mother, but growing up my adoption story was only happy. My parents always made me feel like I was a gift.

I was raised in a loving family, but quite often I felt like the odd one out. I didn't fit in with other children my age. There were ways of doing things in France when I was growing up—ways of looking and being, especially if you are a girl—that felt alien to me.

One of these peculiarities that set me apart was my desire to become a chef. It wasn't only the fact that, for someone raised by professional parents, cooking didn't seem like a respectable job. Nor was it that neither my parents nor I knew anyone who actually did it for a living. The truth is that, in France during the years I was growing up, becoming a chef simply wasn't something a woman would do.

Women cooked, of course. We nurtured and organized and ran households up and down the country, but we didn't put on chef's whites and run kitchens. We didn't open fancy restaurants or win Michelin stars, and we didn't have culinary theories or innovate. We were homemakers, not artists, so that while it was normal for a French girl to want to cook, it was not normal for a French girl to want to be a chef and dream of opening her own restaurant.

For many years, I didn't even know these were the things I wanted. All I knew was that I didn't want what I was supposed to want, a life culminating in marriage and children, around which a job might be discreetly arranged. In the 1970s and '80s, these were the only proper goals for a French woman, so that for a while I thought the problem was France. I'm not French enough, I thought. My genetic heritage was mixed and uncertain, and France, with its severity and purity—with the inflexibility that lurks beneath its founding principles of *liberté*, *égalité*, and *fraternité*—didn't suit me. Only America, truly the land of the free, would save me.

I was half right about this. Moving to the West Coast of America in my early twenties certainly opened up my life in ways that would never have happened in France. But it's not the case that on reaching the United States I suddenly, seamlessly, fit in. I loved San Francisco, but I was still me and the world was still the world.

One of the more depressing of these universals was that, even in America, a restaurant kitchen was still a man's domain. In the first fifteen years of my career, I was yelled at and groped and made to work through injury. I survived horrible business managers and tyrannous head chefs. At the age of forty-five, when I finally opened my first restaurant, it was in the wake of the global financial crisis and I was told that, even in the best of circumstances, I was entering a tough business at a tough time. On top of that, as a woman opening a fine-dining restaurant with vaguely avant-garde ambitions, I was practically laughed out of the room.

I could have tried to change myself. I could have made more effort to knuckle down and conform. I could have, as was suggested to me way back at the beginning, when I had just graduated from college and was thinking of applying to cooking school, checked my ambition and become the manager of a restaurant rather than the chef or the owner. This is what women do; they settle for second, third, fourth best. They fold their ambition into smaller and smaller pieces until it disappears altogether.

It never felt like a choice to me. I was a didn't-fit-in kind of girl who became a didn't-fit-in kind of woman, and as I grew older, I started to understand that everything I've achieved—owning my own restaurant, becoming the first woman chef in the United States to be awarded three Michelin stars, even marrying the woman I loved—was not in spite of these differences but because of them. If I had to describe my motivation in life, the words I would choose would be "curiosity" and "courage." In French we say "*bon courage*," which has the advantage of meaning both "be brave" and "good luck." And when girls approach me for advice, I tell them to be courageous! Be curious! And, above all, to understand that, while success in any field requires a strong vision, to make that vision fly you need other people. Especially since I don't know the story of my genes going back five generations, my security and continuity lies in the strength of the connections I've made with others, and the knowledge that they are everything I have in this world.

A lot of my cooking is inspired by my earliest memories, which are some of the happiest memories I have. I might serve you potatoes roasted in their own soil with a ham broth, and with it the summers I spent on my grandmother's farm. You might taste black trumpet mushrooms with toasted pumpernickel and chickpeas while walking alongside my father and me through the woods, or sit down to smoked oysters and freshly steamed langoustine while joining me at my mother's table for lunch. Perhaps, in these memories, you will find reflections of your own.

Which brings us around to the question of luck. While I

had the good fortune to be adopted by wonderful people, who loved me and gave me a good start in life, the real luck, as I see it, is that I never regarded any circumstance to be the end of the story. Living is moving. Nothing is learned by standing still. We are all works in progress. This is how I see things, good or bad—as an invitation, much like the one I extend to you, now, to come with me, through this open door.

My first birthday with my parents.

PART ONE

One

HOME

One day late in the summer of my twenty-fourth year, I stepped off a plane and took a deep breath. I had never been to San Francisco before, but as I breathed in, I knew instantly, almost violently, and without a shadow of a doubt something that a quarter of a century later I'm still completely convinced of: I was home.

I had left my parents that morning on a station platform in Quimper, northern France, waving to me as my train left for Paris. My brother, Jean-Christophe, was beside them. A day earlier, we had all stood in a church and watched him get married, surrounded by family and friends. That was where I belonged, in a lush farming region of northwest France where I had lived all my life and where my family has roots going back generations. And yet, as my train left the station that day, I was ecstatic. I couldn't wait to get out.

The decision to move to America looked, from the outside, impulsive. My English was imperfect. I had no long-standing friends or relations in the United States. My parents, although well traveled, were chiefly interested in Europe and I had inherited their priorities. And even though I had grown up hooked on American TV shows—primarily *Starsky & Hutch*, those maverick TV cops of the 1970s whom I'd once planned to grow up and turn into—my knowledge of the United States was hazy. I could talk for hours about German reunification, the Polish Solidarity movement, or the long-range fallout of the Second World War on French politics, but I was largely ignorant about the United States. This was partly why I wanted to move there. For some, lack of information is frightening. For me, it has always been energizing.

This draw I feel toward the unknown, and the fundamental curiosity that drives it, is connected to how I came into the world. I have two birth certificates, with a different name and a different birthplace on each. My parents are Allain and Louise Crenn and my brother is Jean-Christophe Crenn, but I'm aware that I have at least two other siblings in the world, neither of whom I have met and about whom I know nothing. And then there is the riddle of my birth parents.

When I left France that hot summer day, I knew these three things about myself: I knew I had been placed in an orphanage at the age of six months. I knew that the name on my birth certificate had been Dominique Michele. And I knew that when my parents first set eyes on me, I had been smiling.

I knew lots of other things, too, of course. I knew I was competitive. I knew I was ambitious. I knew my recently completed degree in economics, undertaken in the absence of any better ideas and largely to please my education-loving parents, wasn't going to be the basis of my career. I knew I loved poetry—especially Baudelaire—for the way it could transfer emotion from one person to another, and I knew I wasn't going to be a poet. The things I had loved as a child revolved around being outside and running around, and at the age of twenty-four nothing much had changed. I couldn't imagine doing a job that kept me hunched over a desk or in an office all day.

I also knew I liked cooking. My love of food was almost too intimate to connect with a career. It was deeply bound up with my love for my family and my relationship with the country I was leaving. To me, France didn't mean Paris or fashion or the Left Bank or the Belle Epoque, although I loved all those things. At mineral level, however, France meant something else: the blazing green countryside and the wild northwest coast. It meant lobster just caught from the sea and vegetables yanked from the earth, dirt still clinging to their roots. There was something about plunging my fingers into the warm summer soil or biting into cold salted butter on fresh bread that affected me the way nothing else did. It would take me a long time to articulate and even longer to accept, but deep down, on that day of departure, I knew I loved France.

Of course, I hated the place, too. The reality of living in France, where tradition is revered to the point of intransigence, is that doing things differently is rarely an option, and even as a child I had known I was different. It wasn't simply that my interests were different from those of my friends. I was different in more profound ways, too. To be adopted is to have a shadow life, to live alongside the outline of What Might Have Been. What if I had stayed with my birth mother? What if another couple had adopted me? What if no one had adopted me and I had grown up in the orphanage? These were thoughts that as a child had the power to flip my stomach. When I boarded the plane that day, it is safe to say the number of things I didn't know about myself—crucial, structural things of a kind that, for most people, go to the heart of who they think they are—outnumbered the things that I did.

It didn't matter. The blank slate of my adoption opened up possibilities for reinvention. And while the details might have been slight, for twenty-four years the story of where I had come from had told me everything I needed to know. I knew the world was wide open and anything could happen.

In the mid-1960s, my parents lived in Garches, a picturesque town near Versailles seven miles west of Paris, because of my dad's job. When I was growing up, my dad moved between various government posts in and around Paris. For a while he worked as the director general of a think tank called the CFPC— Centre de formation des personnels communaux—and later as the secrétaire général in Meudon. At the time of my adoption,

My second birthday, April 7, 1967.

he was the regional representative for Brittany in the French national government and went to work every day at the National Assembly.

This was kind of a big deal. As a child, I was never ashamed or self-conscious of being adopted, mostly thanks to my parents' attitude; they were so open and positive about our adoption, it never occurred to me to be otherwise. I suspect that some of my confidence, however, also came from the fact of who my father was. We weren't wildly rich, but in the communities of my childhood Allain Crenn was a well-respected and connected politician, among whose friends and mentors included Charles de Gaulle. The pair had met in London during the Second

World War, when my father was a volunteer for the French Resistance and de Gaulle was head of the Free French government in exile in Britain. In the 1960s, when de Gaulle was president of France, he and my father remained on friendly terms.

I like to imagine my father as a swashbuckling teenage Resistance hero. But in a quieter way, my parents' decision to adopt my brother and me, two children of obscure origin, was an act of bravery, too. It's worth remembering that 1960s France was not a liberal place. The demonstrations that took place in 1968, and that both of my parents participated in, broke out in part as a response to the stifling conservatism of a society in which the Catholic Church still wielded enormous influence. Even now, France is less progressive than it might superficially seem: legally, gay couples can adopt in France, but in reality it is extremely difficult. Algerians and North Africans face widespread discrimination. In 1966, a couple adopting children who did not look altogether "French" was a broad-minded act.

I never spoke to my parents about their inability to conceive a biological child, but later I found letters that hinted at how difficult it had been. "No baby yet," wrote my mother, painfully, in letters home to her family years before my brother and I were adopted, a sentiment echoed by my father in his own letters. "We hope to expand our family soon," he wrote.

I sometimes think that my father's open-mindedness came in part from having grown up with three sisters. There was a sensitivity to him, an openness to the world and to others that I have always put down to his upbringing as the only boy among women. When my parents adopted my brother and me, they did so with it firmly in mind that it doesn't matter where you come from, or even whether where you come from could ever be known.

In the case of Jean-Christophe, the lack of information about his birth parents was absolute. Jean-Christophe was a little boy with dark hair and chubby cheeks who was impossible not to love and who, my parents were told by the orphanage, had been abandoned at birth by a woman whose name they couldn't disclose. They could, however, tell my parents she was from a wealthy and prominent family in Orsay, near Versailles, and had conceived Jean-Christophe out of wedlock; her family had told her that if she kept the child, they'd disown her. Part of the terms of his abandonment were that the name of his birth mother would never be revealed.

By contrast, my birth mother's surname was on my birth certificate, there was a full file on me at the orphanage—albeit one we weren't permitted to see—and my place of birth was listed as Saint-Germaine-en-Laye, a suburb of Paris. Growing up, I had no reason not to believe this information. Whoever heard of a birth certificate getting it wrong?

The story of my adoption begins when my parents came to the orphanage, looking for a little girl to be a sister for Jean-Christophe. It was another little girl, one of Algerian origin, whom my parents planned to adopt that day. They had already met her and played with her, but that day the director of the orphanage called them into his office, and while they sat anxiously across the desk from him, informed them it had come to light that the little girl had a sibling, a brother, who was elsewhere in the orphanage system. What did they want to do?

This was a terrible dilemma for my parents. They didn't want three children. On the other hand, they didn't think it was right to separate the child from her brother. Reluctantly, they told the orphanage director they didn't think they could take the little girl, and in that moment, both her life and my own were transformed. It was as they were walking out of the orphanage, full of guilt and disappointment, that another child caught their eye. She was less than a year old, smiling and grabbing at their feet as they passed. When they asked the director of the orphanage about her, they were told her name was Dominique. She just got here, the director said.

What happened next is so imbedded in the legend of my adoption that it feels like the beginning of everything. My brother, who at two and a half had accompanied my parents to the orphanage, took one look at me, toddled over, and gave me a big hug while the adults looked on in amazement. I sometimes think that the fierceness with which I love Jean-Christophe is connected, in some deep way, to an idea I have of him as the person who "chose" me.

Breaking to my parents that I was moving to the United States had been a stressful and nerve-racking experience. I didn't want to hurt them. As a young man, my dad had struck out on his own, leaving the family farm to go into politics, but he

Inseparable.

had moved only a few hours away from his parents and would eventually retire back to Brittany. My brother had settled a few miles from my parents' summer home in Locronon. With the exception of my father's sister Josephine, who had emigrated to South Africa, the rest of the family was in France. My desire to go further afield with no definite plans was not one my parents immediately recognized, and although this was a feeling that over the years I had grown used to, it still unsettled me.

As the plane took off, I comforted myself by going over all the things that I knew. I knew how to triage a potato. I knew what a freshly caught lobster smelled like, and how that smell could fizz through one's brain. From my father's example, I knew that the most important thing was to fight for what you believe in and for those you love—even if, like me, you were hell-bent on leaving them. Before leaving France, I had approached various culinary colleges and training schools and been warned I might not be suitable for acceptance. As the plane landed in San Francisco that evening, I knew something else, too, the strength of which, perhaps, no one else knew: that whatever happened next, being told no simply wasn't an option.

Two

THE FARM

My father's first language was Breton, a Celtic dialect that came over to France from Britain in the early Middle Ages and has shared roots with Cornish, Gaelic, and Welsh. It was only when he went to school that he was forced to learn French, a fact that still irritated him decades later. People from Brittany have a particular outlook, informed partly by the inclement weather. They called it *"le crachin Breton,"* the unceasing cold drizzle that comes in from the sea. After centuries of being battered by the waves, wind, and rain that lash the westernmost part of France, the Bretons have evolved into a proud people who, relative to the average French person, can be a little uptight.

My dad was a classic illustration of this. Five foot ten, dark, and very handsome, with kind, brown eyes behind glasses, he had an intensity that drew the eyes of the room to him. When

Papa Crenn.

Maman.

my dad walked into a gathering, he was seen. There was a calmness to him that was much more compelling than the mien of someone seeking attention, and he was also physically robust. When you see those clean-cut military boys, standing politely with poker-straight backs—that's my dad.

Politics was not an obvious career path for a boy from a farm, all of whose forefathers had been farmers. Jean-François Crenn, my father's father, had raised cattle and pigs on a farm in Guimiliau, a tiny Breton village with medieval roots that lay smack-bang in the center of the region. The only time my paternal grandfather left his home for any length of time was to fight in the First World War, when he was decorated for bravery during the Battle of the Somme. When the Second World War broke out, it wasn't surprising that his son volunteered as soon as he could. It was my father's experience of fighting for a country under daily existential threat that, I suspect, turned his ambitions away from farming and toward politics.

In the 1960s, it was common for French families to avoid talk of the war, but this was not the case in our house. Openness was, perhaps, a habit formed by the necessity of discussing the details of our adoption, although I think my parents were probably just naturally open people. But in any case, as far back as I can remember, everything—or almost everything—was up for discussion in my family. I heard about how my dad, at the age of sixteen, had joined the Resistance and operated under the code name Jean Le Bon. I heard about how, as a teenage volunteer, he had undertaken sabotage operations against the Germans. I thrilled to hear the stories of how he later joined something called the FFI, the Forces Françaises de l'Intérieur, and, encouraged by his father, an amateur pilot, learned how to parachute from a plane. The tales always ended the same way, in May 1945, with my father flying in a plane over Denmark when news of the European armistice came through.

The effect of his exploits on my imagination was vivid, but no more so, in a way, than the quieter example set by my mother. My maman is five foot four, very much the elegant French woman, who grew up with six siblings on a potato farm a few miles from my dad's village. The story of how they met was one I loved to hear. My dad had gone out to watch a bicycle race pass through the village when he saw a nineteen-year-old girl with long black hair standing on the other side of the square. After chatting with her for a few moments, he asked her out. To the amazement of everyone in the village who heard this story after the fact, my mother didn't jump to say yes.

My mother was eleven years younger than my dad, and although they both came from respectable farming families, my father was considered the superior catch. A decorated war hero and rising political star, all the best families in the area had him in mind for their daughters. And yet here was my mother, regarding him cautiously and telling him that before she'd go out with him, he'd have to trudge back to the farm with her to meet her father.

This is in part why my dad fell in love with her; my mother

Papa and Maman on their wedding day.

had a mind of her own. "Why her?" people said when they announced their engagement. The answer is he wanted my maman, this ambitious woman who set him straight when she believed he was wrong and would go on to have her own successful career. It always makes me happy to remember this about my dad—that he was willing to work for my mother's affection.

The apartment my parents took me home to in the winter of 1966 was reached by driving through an ornate gate and up a long driveway, with beautiful gardens on either side. Garches is a beautiful town that, like its more famous neighbor, Versailles, is full of grand eighteenth-century buildings and wide, tree-lined boulevards. Our apartment was on the top floor of the town hall, a grace-and-favor residence given to my dad as a perk of his job, and which we had all to ourselves. Outside, the garden was like a private park.

Looking in the mirror can be a complicated business for adopted children, but in February 1966, the Crenn family looked, at a glance, as if we belonged together. My brother, fifteen months older than me, could have been Iranian or maybe Italian. I looked perhaps Algerian or Moroccan, and my parents, although lighter skinned than both of us, had black hair and dark eyes in the Mediterranean style. In almost every picture of the two of us, my brother is hugging me so hard I am half falling down.

Although both of my parents worked, it was my mother who did all the cooking. (My mother also did most of the driving and, because she worked as a financial adviser, oversaw the

My brother and I, playing as always.

1967 in the Jardin des Garches.

family's spending. Of the two of them, she was the more practical parent, leaving my dad to do all the dreaming.) After school or at the weekend, I would accompany her to the market in Garches and she would shop for what we needed that night: on weeknights, a simple dinner of fish or charcuterie, roasted vegetables, and salad, with soup—my dad loved soup—followed by cheese. On the weekends, she would prepare something more elaborate, involving fish or one of her famous seafood platters.

There is no quicker way to understand my parents' divergent personalities than via the way in which they each shopped for food. My mother had an eye for picking the freshest vegetables at the market, and if asked, could talk knowledgeably about the soil and how to make things grow. But those shopping trips were not romantic. They were completely utilitarian and she would stick to her rotation of the same few useful stalls. This was not my approach at all. While she shopped, I would wander off, drawn to the stalls that sold Middle Eastern and North African spices, bags of sumac and Aleppo, cumin and ginger. Even as a young child, I understood that just to inhale the scent of these spices—woody and thick, spicy and fresh—was to travel far beyond one's surroundings. My mother would finish up, call me over, and we would head right home.

When I went shopping with my dad, it was a different story. He would take me to the fish market at Port de Douarnenez, a few miles from my parents' summer home in Brittany, and it was as if we were visiting a museum. The mere fact of getting up before dawn to arrive at the open-air market in time to greet the yellow-booted fisherman as they returned to shore infused the whole expedition with a sense of occasion. My dad would have a list of things my mother had given him to buy, but this was a secondary part of the excursion. The real purpose of the trip was for my dad to talk to the fishermen, and for me to stay close to his side to listen.

My father was fascinated by people who lived on the water. He loved the sense of adventure it required, as well as the courage and skill, and he encouraged me to be interested, too. He wanted to know in granular detail what it was like to be at sea for months at a time. He was interested in the mechanics of fishing—what it took to be successful and how to navigate a storm—but more than that, he was interested in the psychology of the fishermen themselves and how they managed to do a job that most of us would barely last a day at.

For a young child, those early mornings were incredibly evocative. I would luxuriate in the treat of being alone with my father while taking in the smell of the sea and the mist rising off the water. Around us the fishermen yelled out, selling their wares. In French, the word for a wholesale fish market is "*la criée*," which derives from the sound of the men hawking the fish, a tradition going back centuries. My parents believed in Jesus Christ, but for me, the true origin of everything is water, an idea I later realized was informed during the trips to the fish market. In my mind, those dreamy mornings merged with my understanding of evolution into a kind of murky mythology. The sea was where life began.

Eventually, my dad would stop talking and buy something and we would head home, where my maman would take the live lobster or mackerel, mussels or oysters, steam them, and put them straight on a plate. Add some pain de seigle—rye bread— butter, sea salt, a little bit of lemon, and boom! Years later, I would try to make a recipe that drew on the memory of these mornings, a dish that frothed on the plate like the sea, with squid ink meringue and pickled mussels, or tai snapper and sea urchin, depending on the season. It can take an awful lot of work, I have since discovered, to find one's way back to the simple pleasures of childhood.

My early food memories are simple. I remember the fish from the market and I remember my mother's straight-forward home cooking. I remember the smell of the spices and the roasted chestnuts at Christmas. I remember, with the intensity of a child's first encounter with sugar, the wonder of pastries. One summer, while the house in Locronon was being built, we stayed in a small family-owned hotel in a neighboring village, where I ran around the kitchen with my brother and stuffed my face with kouign-amann: an amazing batter cake folded with butter and sugar that is a specialty of that part of Brittany.

We were an informal family, but occasionally my parents had guests round for dinner and then everything changed. My mother would put on a beautiful dress and walk around the house trailing the smell of Chanel perfume. There would be jazz on the record player and chilled seafood piled high on a platter. This was my mother's signature party dish and it was a showstopper: lobster and oysters, shrimp and sea snails, accompanied by a sauce of clarified butter and herbed mayonnaise. It was at once impossibly fancy—the sheer theater of a tower of expensive shellfish—and devastatingly plain, involving very little in the way of gussying up the ingredients. When the guests arrived, it was my job to hand each of them a Kir Breton, a champagne flute of crème de cassis topped with sparkling French cider. Decades later, I would serve a version of this to every guest who sat down in my restaurant, a kind of spritz to the brain that served as a reference to my mother's elegance and hospitality—the very essence of the special occasion.

Those dinner parties of my parents taught me how food could be used to create an atmosphere of glamour and fun, but it was the lower-key food moments that have had a greater effect on my cooking. I have one very clear memory that has taken on almost talismanic proportions. I was about eight or nine and went into the garden at Locronon to pick a tomato from the vine. I must have eaten tomato before, but as far as I'm aware I'd never picked one and eaten it, and after inspecting the fruit, I bit into the flesh as if it were an apple. The juice sprayed, releasing a flavor that was at once sharp and sweet, with the musty undertone that comes from the stalk, and so intense my mind just blew up. As a chef, I have always thought of the tomato as the test of how good a simple ingredient can be, an irreducible unit of flavor that reminds one that food is a sharpener of life. When I cook, I want everything to have the shocking immediacy of that first picked tomato.

The summer house in Locronon in Brittany was a six-hour drive from Garches and about six miles inland from the sea. If you had to imagine a stereotypical French village, Locronon would be it, a picture-perfect medieval village popular as a location with French filmmakers and featuring a Gothic church, cobbled streets, and stunning views of bucolic farmland. One of these farms was my grandmother's.

Growing up, I spent far more time in the suburbs of Paris than on vacation in Brittany, but if you were to ask me which part of the world takes up the most space in my mind, there would be no contest: from the earliest age, rural Brittany is where I felt truly at home, partly through an instinctive love for the land, but mainly because of my grandmother, Hervelyn.

It is easy, looking back, to romanticize one's childhood summers. They seemed to go on forever and involve uninterrupted months of cloudless blue skies, during which my brother and I practically lived outdoors. Perhaps there were days of boredom and rain, but I don't remember them. What I remember is that for two months every summer, we stayed on my grandmother's farm and life was as good as it gets.

People were inclined to find my grandmother—my mother's mother—scary, and although she didn't scare me, I could see why. She was six feet tall and a formidable organizer. She had raised seven children, and after her husband, my maternal grandfather, died when I was about four, had carried on running her potato farm alone. My mother is quiet and not judgmental, a person of courage, but discreetly so. Hervelyn, on the other hand, was like a rural French version of the Godfather. She could be witty and fun, particularly when she was telling us stories, but there's no question that when she spoke people sat up and listened. She and I instinctively got along, a feeling aided by the fact that I was very well-behaved on the farm. It was easy for me; I liked being there.

She lived in a big farmhouse, with a large open area downstairs, at the center of which was a hearth and a fire. I slept in a room with my cousins and had to trek downstairs and outside to the toilet. On both my grandparents' farms—we visited my paternal grandfather's dairy farm, too, although less frequently— the toilets were in an outhouse, and although eventually they were brought inside, for most of those summers of my childhood we lived in what felt like another century. In the morning, we got up and headed out to the fields and stayed out until the sun started to set.

Potatoes are not a glamorous product and harvesting them is hard, sweaty work. On my grandmother's farm, there was a machine that went back and forth, plucking the potatoes from the soil then spitting them out for the three or four people on each side of the machine to rake through, sorting for defects. I was still very young when I was allowed to join in with the

sorting. If a potato came up rotten or with too many roots growing out of it, I had to throw it in one pile, while unblemished
specimens would go in another. My brother never took to this
task, but from the get-go, I loved it. To a young child, helping
out in the exclusive company of adults can feel like a tremendous honor and responsibility, and I loved the feeling of working with others, all intensely focused on a single task.

I also loved the sheer physicality of what we were doing. As
an experience, helping out in the fields was one of sensory overload. The people around me were mostly men, my uncle and
local farmhands, and when I looked up from the potatoes I
would see the sun on their faces, the sweat pouring down, while
their hands raked through the black soil and the air shimmered
with heat. It was like a painting by an old master.

At lunchtime, my grandmother would come out from the
house into the fields carrying provisions for lunch. We would
drop down onto the ground while my uncle opened a knife, cut
the bread, spread the butter, and hacked off a piece of saucisson
to make a rough sort of sandwich. Some days, my grandmother
would make a stew and bring it out to us, and we'd drag the
bread through the sauce and meat. I can still see it: the hot food,
the soup, the stew, the sun—the unimaginable intensity of all
these factors combined.

Not surprisingly, my affection for the farm didn't wane as
I grew older. To a young child, having the run of a farm with
all that mud and freedom was a powerful and very basic attraction. Later, in high school, when my friends started to ask me

to stay in town over the summer, or go with them on club-bing vacations to Ibiza, I never wanted to go. I loved my friends. But after hanging out with them for a while, I would always get restless and jittery. I had a sense I wasn't exactly like them. Their preoccupation with the hierarchies of high school didn't interest me and I liked being with older people, to the extent that I sometimes felt I'd been born into the wrong generation. Years later, though my brother was off listening to his music and my cousins had their own interests, all I still wanted, every summer, was to pick potatoes and talk with the guys in the fields.

If I were sentimental, I'd say this attraction to Brittany was in my blood, but of course this can't be the case. Not a single strand of my DNA comes from northwest France. Those blood-lines going back five generations aren't mine. And yet the land felt so powerful to me that, as a child, even though I knew I was adopted, the only way I was able to express my strength of feel-ing for the farm was to say it was "in my blood."

What I understand now is that "blood" in this context can be a metaphor simply for that which we hold dearest. Most of us are far too quick to define ourselves in the narrowest terms. How, as a human, did you become you? Did you simply inherit a genetic package from your parents? Are you who you are be-cause of where you were born and how you were raised? I love my parents but I don't think they made me, just as I don't think my birth mother was entirely responsible, either. I think we are more than the sum total of our genes and experiences.

May Day with my family in Brittany.

When my dad filled my head and heart with stories of how he fought to defend the land of his birth, I felt myself swell with pride and belligerence, and I automatically claimed the land as mine, too. In a strange way, my allegiance to Brittany seemed more powerful for not being in my blood. I wasn't genetically programmed to love this particular place; I loved it through a combination of happenstance and choice, and that very randomness—the fact that I ended up where I did— was an alignment so implausible as to seem more like destiny.

Three

AN EDUCATION

When I was six years old, my dad's job changed and we moved from Garches to the neighboring town of Meudon, where we were given an elegant house that bordered the town hall on one side and an orphanage on the other. Meudon is an interesting little city presided over by a royal chateau once favored by the son of Louis XIV. The artist Auguste Rodin came from Meudon, as did Rabelais, the sixteenth-century satirist who wrote a line I have always been fond of: "A child is a fire to be lit, not a vase to be filled." After a few years, my dad changed jobs again and my parents bought a condo in Meudon with wonderful views toward Paris. Since starting school, I had become very busy. I played handball, eventually becoming the captain of my school team. I competed in judo, soccer, and tennis, as well as other sports. I was good at sprints, mainly the 100 and 200 meters,

June 1970, five years old.

and discovered that long-distance running wasn't for me. The fast and the furious suited me better. I realized that I was very competitive and I liked to win.

The only athletic pursuit to which I didn't take was ballet. Oh god, I tried. My parents sent me to classes from the age of about six and I kept going for almost three years. It was partly that I had very short hair and glasses and felt out of place among the other ballerinas. But even without that, the dance didn't interest me. I could enjoy the music, but ballet was way too proper for me, and instead of doing the steps I would mess around until the teacher grew furious. Eventually, I dropped out.

By and large I was a well-behaved kid. I wasn't the best student, but I had a good memory and was diligent in class, partly out of a natural desire to please, and partly out of calculation: the better my grades and behavior, the greater license I had to do what I wanted to do. The only time I got into any real trouble was when I was protecting my brother. Jean-Christophe is older than me, but of the two of us, I have always been the more assertive. He is very kind, generous, and loving, and much softer than I am. If I ever saw him being bullied at school I would jump right in and start fighting. "You can't do that," the principal would say after I'd been sent to his office. But when I got home, my dad was usually on my side.

One day, out of the blue, my mother started bleeding. When she went to the doctor, she was told she had an internal abscess and would have to be admitted to the hospital for treatment. She would end up staying for almost three weeks, and after being discharged was incapacitated at home for a further two months. My father, brother, and I had to fend for ourselves.

Of my parents, my mother might have been the quieter of the two, but she was the engine of our house. If I idolized my

The face of a serious chef.

dad as someone who knew more than anyone else in the world, I recognized my mother as the one who got things done. She was no-nonsense, practical, efficient, and kind, and we all knew she held everything together. When she got sick, we were completely at sea.

Part of the problem was my dad. He was interested in food and had a good palate, but I have to be honest: he was a terrible cook. He would do vaguely culinary things like bring a whole leg of Jambon de Bayonne back from holiday in Spain and hang it in our basement to cure, disappearing before dinner every evening and returning a moment later with a plate piled with slices of ham. But when it came to actually cooking, he was hopeless. In the days after my mother was admitted to hospital, he struggled to feed my brother and me. One night, he served us raw beets with the skin still on.

For years I had been watching my mother in the kitchen, just as she had learned to cook at her mother's side. I knew how to shop at the market—that the main thing was to keep things simple and focus on good, fresh ingredients. And I knew what my dad liked. And so, at nine years old, I took charge of the kitchen. One afternoon I got back from school and tentatively started devising some menus. A little soup; some vegetables and grilled meats; a little salad and a cheese platter with charcuterie. It didn't need to be much—my dad and my brother's needs were very plain—but it had to be better than a TV dinner. At the end of the night, before he went to bed, I would make my dad a pot of chamomile tea.

It was a difficult time. My dad was working very hard and would often come home right before dinner, eat, and be wiped out for the rest of the evening. He was, I knew, tremendously worried about my mother, and going to visit her in the hospital was stressful. At home, although the rest of the family rallied round and gave us support, the house felt small and dark in my mother's absence. The most painful thing, however, wasn't worrying for myself, or even missing my maman, but watching my parents' worry for each other. There is nothing more unsettling to a young child than the collapse of parental infallibility.

I asked my mother about this period recently and the first thing she said was, "Yes, that's when you took over the household so well." Perhaps in some families, a nine-year-old cooking for the family would have been considered odd. What I did in the kitchen during those weeks barely qualified as cooking—it was assembly more than anything else—but through a trying time, making food for my family kept me going. It felt to me like the simplest and most tangible way to show care, in a language I, at the age of nine, couldn't have articulated any other way. When after three months my mother returned to good health and the kitchen, I felt tremendous relief and also a sense of accomplishment. More than that, I felt something I had never felt so clearly before: purpose.

As I got older, I started to travel more widely. As a family, we went on holiday to Spain and Martinique. I loved the Basque country, the fatty taste of the ham we ate there, the sense of Spanish history. We went on hiking trails through the Pyrenees, wrapped up against the cold, where I would take great gulps of clean mountain air and thrill to how different it was from the sea. Back at Locronon, we spent long days on the beach, returning to the house where my dad would retire to his atelier, a small workshop in the garden where he did all his painting. My dad's day job was challenging and interesting, but I sometimes think he truly came into himself only when he was at his easel. He had no formal training as an artist, but he was good and his paintings were very personal. One day, he painted

Four years old, hiking in Lourdes.

a canvas with beautiful white flowers. He said that as he'd worked on it he'd been thinking of me.

Some of the trips I went on were better than others. One summer, my brother and I were sent to La Colonie de Vacances, a kind of summer camp in the Vendée on the west coast of France. After a week, I wanted to get out. I didn't like the director of the place, although I couldn't put my finger on why. I have always trusted my instincts, however, and when I don't like something, I tend to speak up. When my parents came to visit, I told them there was something about this guy that gave me the creeps. That's all it took. They pulled my brother and me out and drove us straight home.

Another summer, when I was eleven, my brother and I went on a student exchange trip with our school, to a school in the south of England. The school was in Farnborough, Hampshire, and each of us was put up by a different host family. A few days into the trip, one of my brother's friends was caught stealing from his hosts, and although Jean-Christophe was not implicated, I was informed by the teacher that, because of his association with the thief, he was to be sent home, too.

This seemed to me a monstrous injustice. The next day, when the perpetrator and my brother were due at the school early, I was waiting for them in the courtyard at 7:00 a.m. Without thinking, I ran up to the boy who had caused all the trouble and started to beat him up. The teachers could hardly get me off him. Eventually, Mme Gremier, our English teacher, pulled me off the boy, and I was taken to the head teacher's office.

Freezing cold water at the beach in Brittany.

When they got my dad on the phone, I could barely get the words out. "Dad, Jean-Christophe—" I said.

"I know," he said. "I know the story. Are you okay?"

"Yes," I said. "Are you mad at me?"

"No," he said. My dad always approved when I stood up for my brother. "You did the right thing."

Growing up, overall, I was happy at home. I was happy at school. I loved my parents and was secure and had friends. I was doing well in every area of my life. And yet, as I entered my teens, I started to see myself as someone who didn't really fit in.

It is hard to pin down where a feeling of not belonging originates when it doesn't correspond to the obvious things. It's true that I had some unresolved feelings about my adoption, and how I couldn't find a reflection of myself, anywhere. I was always looking at faces, interested in the physical traits that they had and wondering if I might have them, too. At the same time, if anyone ever tried to claim me, I would shrink in horror. Strangers would occasionally stop me in the store to speak Arabic, assuming I was of North African or Middle Eastern descent, and I would be filled with indignation. It wasn't that I didn't want to be those ethnicities, but rather that it felt like a negation of my life. "I'm not you!" I would rage in my head, in that moment claiming my parents and my right to be from Brittany.

And, as I approached my teens, it's also possible that my balance was upset as my sexuality started to come into question. I had always looked slightly different than the other girls, favoring short, boyish haircuts, and as early adolescence drew closer, my tastes started to feel at odds with those of the people around me.

In the late 1970s, few people in French public life were openly gay; it wasn't spoken of on TV or referred to in newspapers, except in the context of a sex scandal. And while my parents were liberal in some ways, our social milieu was overwhelmingly straight, white, and Catholic. I had no idea that a wife might be in my future; all I had was the vague sense that my style, interests, and enthusiasms weren't quite right for a girl my age. I also had a feeling that it was something my parents wouldn't understand.

There were other things that set me apart, too. Looking back, it seems to me that if I felt different from my peers, it wasn't only because I didn't know who my birth parents were or because I had a crush on Olivia Newton-John. It was also because I had unusual interests for someone of my age. I preferred talking to adults rather than other children. In spite of my friends, I was a bit of a loner. I sometimes looked at the other kids—particularly those who boasted about going on ski trips or other expensive holidays—and thought they didn't think for themselves. I couldn't find myself in those groups, where the girls in particular always seemed a bit vacant. And I was a political junkie, which no other eleven-year-old I knew was.

Every night at the dinner table, my dad talked to me about politics. He knew I was interested in political history and would tell me about the figures he admired, such as Simone Veil, the French health minister and survivor of Auschwitz who in the mid-1970s passed the first abortion laws in France. He told me about Simone de Beauvoir and sketched an outline for me of French feminist history. He talked about Coco Chanel, who'd once had a house not far from our old place in Garches.

When we talked, it was never like he was trying to impose his views on me. The point of our conversations was to wake up my curiosity, and after he talked, it was my turn. I sometimes think there is no greater gift a parent can give to their child than to listen—to really listen.

After a few years of absorbing my dad's talk about politics, I found it wasn't enough for me to simply listen. I was ravenous for more information about the world and I wanted to get out there and see it. My dad had some good friends in Warsaw whom he had met through his political connections, and when I was twelve, I did something truly eccentric: I begged my parents to let me travel to see them.

It is extraordinary, looking back, that I was permitted to take this trip. This was in the late 1970s, when Poland was still under Communist rule and often on the TV news owing to its cycles of unrest and authoritarian crackdown. Generally in life I like to be in the middle, where I can get ideas from both sides. But political extremism fascinates me and I was obsessed with learning what life was like behind the crumbling Iron Curtain. Please, please, please, I asked my dad, can I go to Warsaw? Astonishingly, after enough pestering, he said yes, as long as my brother went with me. And so a twelve-year-old and a fourteen-year-old boarded a train in Paris bound for Communist Poland.

I don't know what I expected. And my mind still boggles at the idea that my dream vacation, at that age, was to spend almost twenty-four hours on a train while it chugged toward a totalitarian state. At the time, however, I just threw myself into it and let the adventure unfold. The train was a sleeper. My brother took the bottom bunk and I took the top. That first afternoon, we sat playing cards and looking through the window as the flat, European farmland sped by, before retiring to our bunks for the night. The idea of sleeping on a train was impossibly exciting.

Very early the next morning, we were woken by sharp noises. The train had reached the border between West and East Germany, and as I pulled back the curtains, I saw a line of soldiers with rifles and German shepherds. They were shouting as they boarded the train: "Passports! Passports! Passports!" My brother and I fumbled with our paperwork, hearts pounding, but nobody raised the slightest objection to the passage of two unaccompanied minors. Eventually, the train resumed its journey.

I found the experience of seeing the world anew, stripped of every certainty, completely and utterly mind-blowing. Our dad's friend was there to meet us on the platform in Warsaw, and the first thing I asked him about was the wagons we had seen from the train with USSR stenciled on the side. He explained that in spite of severe food shortages in Poland, the country was obliged to send a great deal of its farms' produce to Russia. "How do you guys live?" I asked, and when we returned to his house, he opened a trap door and showed his family's stash of black market food. It was like something out of a movie.

It was also an early lesson in something I would come to better understand years later: food is politics. When a government wants to suppress its people, the first thing it does is go after the food—just look at the famine in France before the Revolution. If you control the food, you control the people, and this can be as true of Western democracies as of repressive regimes. Industrial farming and the might of the sugar and fast-food lobbies don't exert the same control as a totalitarian government, but they are still hugely powerful. Nutrition informs behavior, and a badly nourished populace, like a badly educated one, is compromised in its political will.

After that first trip to Warsaw, I revisited Poland many times, right up to the 1989 elections, when the Communist order started to crumble and Lech Walesa and his Solidarity movement entered the government. By then, I had totally fallen in love with the place and the Polish people. One of my first boyfriends was Polish. I went to a Polish wedding, where the food was terrible. Like German food, Polish food is all sausage and potato, and not my kind of thing at all. But I loved the country and went back every time I had the chance.

I am still amazed by the bravado of that first trip. If Poland fascinated me, it was because of something I wouldn't have been able to articulate at the time, but that I can now identify as an interest in the dynamics of freedom. On that student exchange trip to England, before my brother was sent home, some English boys playing soccer in the street invited me to join them. I was completely flat-chested, and with my short, dark hair it was obvious to me that they thought I was a boy. For a moment, I hesitated, wondering if I should point out their error. Then I ripped off my shirt, ran out into the street, and for the space of an hour, ran around playing soccer in the sun, as free as anything in the world, as free as the boys.

Four

THE BEST SANDWICH
IN THE WORLD

y father had a best friend who was a food critic, which is a very good best friend to have. Albert Coquil wrote for a big regional newspaper in Brittany called *Le Télégramme* and reviewed restaurants all over the country.

There are different kinds of food critics. There are the ones who revel in the takedown, the cruelty of mocking a kitchen found not up to scratch. There are the ones who know nothing about food and just like to make jokes, and the ones who come in with a political agenda. A restaurant may be cut down to size for being too expensive, too female, too different, too much, none of which may have anything to do with the food.

And then there are the critics like Albert, who know everything about food and restaurant culture, but wield that knowledge responsibly and with a generous heart. Albert never indulged in the takedown. He knew how much work went into even a failing restaurant and still insisted on treating it with respect. If he thought a restaurant wasn't good enough, he simply declined to review it. This omission delivered a gentle message to the chef, who understood implicitly what it meant.

We were lucky; Albert often took my parents with him when he was reviewing. Even luckier, they sometimes took me. Occasionally, we would go to somewhere fancy in Paris, like Le Taillevent, the three-starred Michelin restaurant in the 8th arrondissement, founded in 1946 and named after the first French chef to have written a cookbook. "Taillevent," the alias of Guillaume Tirel, was a cook to the Court of France in the fourteenth century and published a compendium of recipes called *Le Viandier*.

I loved these esoteric facts, and I loved the posh outings. But even more than these things, I loved going with Albert and my parents to the restaurants of Brittany, many of which had Michelin stars, where I was able to see local ingredients given the star treatment. One of these outings was to Jean-Pierre Crouzil, a Michelin-starred restaurant named after the owner. Everything I ate that night summoned the flavor of Brittany: shallots, *reduction*, lemon, vinegar, seaweed, mussels, oysters, langoustines—in short, the ocean. I remember marveling at how all the disparate elements on the plate had a purpose, coming together with a seamless complexity. I had eaten good, plain food before, and I had eaten at fancy restaurants. This, however, was something else; food that was simultaneously surprising and deeply familiar. I had no idea this could even be done. I was completely and utterly fascinated.

I was also fascinated by Albert's job, and as we ate, I would bombard him with questions. How did he go about reviewing a restaurant? What were the criteria? How did he decide if an experience was good, bad, or indifferent? Albert, who, in spite of being very well-known, was still very kind, gave my questions long, patient thought. He told me some funny stories about how his presence in a restaurant could throw a kitchen into turmoil. He relived some of his greatest meals. And then he said something I would never forget: that when he reviewed a restaurant, it was less a question of whether he liked or disliked the food than it was about trying to understand the chef's story.

When I thought about my conversation with Albert, I couldn't understand what he'd meant. A chef's story can't make up for a bad meal, after all. Although the idea that the chef's point of view—where he came from and what he was trying to say—dictates everything from the quality of the service to the ambience of the restaurant to the composition and execution of the menu sort of made sense, it sounded very theoretical to me. You could have the fanciest restaurant in the world, Albert said, but if its mission is to turn out high-end dishes by rote—to throw out just another grilled turbot—nothing on the plate will sing. What, I wondered, might a plate that sang in the way Albert described look like?

I was fourteen years old and didn't know what to do. I loved school, although I got bored very easily. I liked literature. I loved philosophy. I didn't like math. I was good at English. I didn't like German. I was good at sports and continued to compete on all sorts of teams. I got nervous before exams, but was generally good under pressure. I loved cooking and I still loved *Starsky & Hutch*.

For a while, I imagined I might become a photographer. I'm very visual and I liked the idea of fixing a moment in time—of capturing an instant and preserving the memory forever. A photographer is almost the exact opposite of a chef; once enjoyed, a good meal, like a good stage play, can never be revisited, whereas a photograph can live on forever. And yet a good meal shares the properties of a photograph to the extent that it is focused entirely on a passing experience. Creating a good menu, like taking a good photo, is about trapping your guests in the moment.

My parents believed in the importance of education, but beyond that they were pretty relaxed. My brother and I weren't expected to become lawyers or doctors. As long as we were settled and happy, we could do what we liked. Or rather, we could do what we liked within the constraints of the French educational system. The protocols governing higher education back then were so strict and narrow that you could find yourself, at the age of fifteen, making decisions that could potentially govern what you did for the rest of your life. This is exactly what happened to me when, in my midteens, I decided to drop math. It was a decision based on what seemed like sensible criteria—I wasn't very good at math—but it had the bizarre consequence many years later of effectively ruling out the possibility of my becoming a photographer. In France, if you want to become a high-ranking politician, you have to attend the Institut d'Études Politiques in Paris. And if you want to become a successful photographer, you have to attend a school like the École Nationale Supérieure Louis-Lumière, for which you needed a degree in math to gain entrance. There was often only one route into any given profession, and if you didn't take it, there was no other way in.

My father, I think, would have been pleased if I'd decided to follow him into politics, or gone in my mother's direction, toward finance, but neither of these things interested me. My main interests, apart from sports and photography, were running around outside on the farm and cooking. Neither of these enthusiasms, however, seemed to fit what my parents would have called a proper job, that is, something professional rather than vocational. I would have to keep on thinking.

It was something I'd like to have discussed with my grandmother. While my brother had stopped hanging out on the farm in his early teens, my enthusiasm for the place never wavered, right up until the day, three years earlier, when my grandmother had been admitted to hospital. The first time we visited her we got a terrible shock. She appeared to have shrunk, her six-foot frame tiny under the blankets, her strength whittled down to an unimaginable frailty. I don't remember what I said to her that day—all I remember is worrying about my maman and asking if she was okay—but I do remember she knew I had come into the room. At eleven, I couldn't really process her death and didn't grieve for my grandmother in any recognizable way. But memories of my summers on the farm became more precious. I had always looked up to her as a strong woman who wouldn't let anyone tell her what to do, and whose advice to me had been "be yourself." In those fraught days of adolescence, I needed her strength and confidence to help me figure out what being myself actually meant.

I can't say my grandmother was an obvious feminist role model. That kind of language would have been alien to her and she ran her farm alone out of necessity, not choice. Over the years, however, her toughness had seeped into me, as had her no-nonsense approach to running a business and the grace with which she managed her staff. My grandmother was kind, but she knew what she wanted and she wasn't afraid to give a command. When, eventually, I ran my own kitchen, I realized I had a leadership model reaching back into my earliest memories.

But in the meantime, I still didn't know what I was going to do with my life. In spite of my chats with Albert and all those enjoyable trips with him to review restaurants, I had never fully connected the experience of eating good food with the job of the person who created it. I could barely name a chef, let alone differentiate their styles. Apart from my enthusiasm for my mother's home cooking, I had no idea of what my individual tastes might be, or what could be achieved outside of classic French cooking. That all changed one evening in my late teens, when I was on vacation with my parents in the south of France. We had dinner reservations at Michel Bras, a Michelin-starred restaurant in the remote village of Laguiole, 125 miles north of Toulouse. I was excited to be going to such a celebrated restaurant. But I had no real idea of what was coming my way.

We got to the restaurant in the late afternoon, with the golden light bouncing off the windows. Inside, there was a sense of quietness that went deeper than the mere hush of the dining room. The restaurant was located in a small hotel that Bras had inherited from his parents. As a child, he had grown up in the hotel's restaurant kitchen, where his mother, unusually, had been the chef. Before Bras took over, the restaurant had been known by the name of the hotel—Lou Mazac. In 1982, after it was awarded its first Michelin star, it was known by the name of the chef. Ten years later, Bras would open another eponymous restaurant that would become one of the great dining destinations of the world, a structure of glass, granite, and chrome that sat on a plateau with stunning views over Aubrac.

That night at the hotel, I got to taste Bras' recently invented signature dish—the gargouillou de jeunes legumes—a medley of vegetables, plants, herbs, and flowers that involved up to eighty distinct elements and that came to him, he has said, during a run in the countryside in June 1978.

It's not just that the gargouillou used ingredients in a way I had never seen in cooking before, in a direct reflection of the land around the restaurant. Or that it featured touches that would become standard, such as the smear, or the "spoon drag," the technique of spreading a sauce across a plate. It's that the gargouillou did something I didn't know was permitted in fine dining: replacing the traditional meat or cream-heavy dish with stalks, shoots, leaves, and grains in an explosion of color, flavor, and texture. The plate in front of me that evening was like nothing I had ever seen. It was simultaneously as light as a feather and groaning with ingredients. Edible flowers! Vegetables so vibrant they were almost neon! Endive, chickweed, salsify, pink radish, chervil, nasturtium, and Welsh onion. It was mind-boggling to imagine how Bras had managed to assemble all these elements into a unified whole, but they were somehow perfectly balanced, a microcosm of the natural world on the plate. As I ate, I marveled not only at the taste of the food and the joy of the presentation, but, as Albert did, at the story that was being told by the chef. For the first time, I understood what he'd meant when he'd said the experience of eating in a restaurant was about more than the cooking itself. The entire experience seemed to me somehow poetic.

One has to be careful with that sort of statement, I know. The word "poetry" sets people off, even when it's used in strict context. Calling a restaurant poetic is asking for trouble, and yet that is how it appeared to me that night. It wasn't just the beauty of the food and the head rush of fresh flavors. It was the tempo of a dining room in which service was an almost Kabuki-like spectacle of grace and movement. The restaurant felt like an invitation to slow down and pay attention. Decades before the slow-cooking movement took off, it was there in the little restaurant in Laguiole.

Years later, friends tried to persuade me to accompany them on a trip back to Michel Bras—Chef Bras had become world-famous by that time—but I wouldn't. I was afraid of interfering with the memory. Of all the restaurants I visited in my childhood and adolescence, it was Michel Bras that I remembered most vividly and it was the chef himself to whom, early on in my cooking, I would make the most references. I don't mean that I tried to cook like him. Rather, that I tried to think like him. Michel Bras taught me about integrating the world around you—nature, the poetry of the outside—into your cooking.

The only other chef who struck me with similar force in those years was Olivier Roellinger, whose restaurant in Cancale, Brittany—although very different from Bras—made a similar virtue of putting the world on the plate. If you walked around Cancale before dining at Le Relais Gourmand, the history of the town, a fishing port known as the oyster capital of Brittany, you would soon see, was relived on the menu. Those two chefs offered me a vision of what cooking might be that wasn't just going to cooking school and learning the dishes. It was about reflecting the integrity of your surroundings. It was about making the ingredients speak to the experience of being alive and reveling in the life of the natural world around you. I knew how to cook, but this was something else. It combined the storytelling element of photography with the physical pleasures of the natural world and the stringencies of a conventional profession. It hadn't occurred to me before that being a chef might be a possible or even a desirable goal. Now I started to wonder.

I was making sandwiches. It was my job for the summer during my last year of high school and I was phenomenally good at it. I'd had summer jobs before, the worst being a sales assistant in a department store, where I stood around all day trying not to go mad with boredom, and the best being helping out in the kitchen at a tennis club. Toward the end of high school, my maman heard about a job through her connections at the city council, making sandwiches for low-income kids at a summer camp. And there it was, the perfect fit.

My favorite sandwich, then as now, is a perfectly cooked baguette with a touch of butter, cornichons, maybe a slice of cheese or saucisson, or a little smoked fish. The classic, in other words.

The key to a sandwich is the bread. The bread is the connector and it should be as fresh as possible; a crisp, crusty baguette is heaven on earth. The other thing to remember when you're making a sandwich is that less is more. When I made sandwiches that summer, I was careful to layer the flavor. I knew it was crucial to take care of every ingredient and understand it had a place in the mix. You can't just slice the bread and throw any old thing in there. I made sandwiches that summer as if my life depended on it, and news of their quality spread. By the end of the season, the staff at the summer camp would queue up to get a sandwich every lunchtime alongside the kids.

It wasn't merely the creative labor of putting together the ingredients I enjoyed, but the feeling I got from the idea I was nurturing others. The whole experience threw into relief just how much greater the pleasure of cooking was than, say, the satisfaction I got from studying.

On the other hand, I wasn't about to just run off to join a kitchen—not least because in France, no such romantic pathway exists. Had I turned up at the service entrance to a Michelin-starred restaurant in Paris offering to peel potatoes with a view to becoming a chef, I would have been yelled at to go away and come back in ten years, when I'd paid my dues slogging through cooking school and a bunch of lowlier restaurants. I couldn't see a future for myself in an office, but neither could I see any immediate way to becoming a chef. I could have applied to cooking school at that stage, but from the earliest age my parents had drummed it into me that you didn't get anywhere in life without a degree. And so while I dreamed of the gargouillou, I applied to study economics at a university in the city. It might at least buy me a few years to judge whether my enthusiasm for cooking was a phase.

I wasn't a terrible student. I was still bad at math, but I liked looking at the broader picture of economic theory, which if you squinted hard enough was as much of an art as a science. I was diligent, as I always had been with schoolwork, but for the first time in my life I also had a lot of age-appropriate fun. Before college, a lot of my friends had been older than me. Now I kicked back and went out with kids my age just to have a good time.

I loved to go dancing, and there was no club in late 1970s Paris like Les Bains-Douches, a modish venue in the center of the city built on the site of a ninth-century bathhouse and with a door policy that would have put Studio 54 to shame. Inside we went wild, dancing all night before jumping into the Moroccan-tiled pool in the middle of the club, only drying off as we walked home in the early morning sun.

After three years, I graduated with a decent bachelor's degree, not a single element of which had really excited me. Meanwhile, my interest in food hadn't abated. For the first time, I tentatively mentioned to my parents my interest in becoming a chef, and it was met with baffled silence. Over the years, my parents had noted the enthusiasm with which I tackled any cooking project and the thrill I got from something as simple as shopping in the market. They had heard me give Albert the third degree and knew that I loved discussing food as much as politics. But they were also at a loss. I suspect that, consciously or otherwise, they may have felt that a passion for cooking should be fitted in around a conventional career—like my father's passion for painting—rather than be a career in itself. They never pressured me to reconsider, and, whatever I did, they said, they were behind me 100 percent. But I could tell that they didn't really understand. To them, it looked like a risky career path.

It was risky. I didn't know how to go about becoming a chef, but I knew that in France at least, it would be difficult. I started calling culinary schools. They were uniformly discouraging. How about going into management, one suggested. Women do very well front of house, said another. I wondered if things might be different if I applied to the famous cooking schools in Lausanne, Switzerland, but the response from those schools was equally lukewarm. Women did all the drudge work of cooking at home, but when it came to restaurant culture, the role of the chef as artist was reserved for men.

I don't know what I expected exactly. I had lived in France all my life and knew the way the country worked. The conventions governing institutions, particularly those regarded as gatekeepers to French patrimoine, including language, literature, and cuisine, are chiseled into stone and fiercely defended. There are the way things are done and have always been done and will be done, god willing, evermore. In the entire history of French cooking, only twenty female chefs have been awarded Michelin stars, and still today I have never been so aware of that fact.

I was angered by the response of the cooking schools. My parents had raised my brother and me to believe we could do anything, and for the first time I found myself at a disadvantage for being a girl. If I'm honest, however, a tiny part of me was also relieved to find my way in France blocked. All through my teens I'd dreamed of going to America. Every movie, every pop song, and advertising image from the United States reinforced the idea that it was a country in which anything could happen. And as I entered my twenties, I couldn't shake the feeling that I was in the wrong place.

This wasn't just about becoming a chef. And while I might not have known exactly what I was looking for, I had a hunch I'd never find it in France. Had the culinary schools welcomed me with open arms, I suspect a small part of me might have been horrified. It would have given me no pretext to leave.

I don't meant to be flippant in regard to culinary schools. But I think to be a master of the culinary arts it's necessary to study the history, philosophy, and politics of food. If you want to be a chef, or even a manager, then you should have that academic background, and the sad thing is, it's not always a big part of the culinary education. And then to actually learn to cook? I think you need to be working. Most cooking schools, to my mind, are a waste of time and money. You learn better on the job.

So, the summer after graduating, after the cold reception from culinary schools, I started to self-educate. I read *The Physiology of Taste*, Jean Anthelme Brillat-Savarin's brilliant Enlightenment-era philosophy of gastronomy, in which he famously stated: "Tell me what you eat and I shall tell you what you are." I started reading culinary magazines and learning about food culture outside France. I read with interest about California cuisine and its reconstitution of rustic French cooking. I read about a chef named Jeremiah Tower, an early champion of the organic movement, who left Chez Panisse, the iconic restaurant in Berkeley opened in 1971 by food activist Alice Waters, to start his own restaurant, Stars. Tower, I noted, hadn't gone to cooking school, either.

Once I decide on a goal, I like to move fast. I knew what I wanted. Why prevaricate for decades trying to get there? If I stayed in France, I reasoned, my only realistic course of action would be to beg for an apprenticeship at a kitchen, but the chances of my rising from there to own my own restaurant, or even to run my own team, with less than several decades' experience, seemed extremely slim.

In France, I couldn't see a way forward. There would be no shortcuts, no loopholes, no chance of slipping the net or rising above my station. If you were young, inexperienced, and on top of that a woman in the French culinary world, there simply wasn't a space for you.

I would have to find another way. I had an Iranian-American boyfriend at the time who I'd met in Paris and who, the summer of my brother's wedding, told me he was moving back to San Francisco. I didn't know anything about San Francisco, other than that it wasn't too far from LA. It hardly mattered, and I jumped at the chance to travel with him. I had no job, no lodging, no friends, and no visa, but I didn't care. Whatever San Francisco was, it had one major advantage over all my other options: it wasn't in France.

Five

SAN FRANCISCO

San Francisco was a different city in 1989. I knew something of the civil rights movements that had taken place there in the 1970s, and of course I associated the city with the hippie movement of the 1960s. What surprised me was how much of that history still resonated. Walking around the city in those early days, I was in a state of almost constant amazement. I would stroll down a street in the Mission, or browse the stores of Haight-Ashbury, looking at the people around me with my mouth half open and my heart pounding.

To me, "freedom" had always meant big political movements: the freedom of the French from fascism after the Second World War, or of the Polish from Communism thirty years later. I had never given much thought to freedom in connection with personal choice. Now, wandering around San Francisco, what I saw was a freedom I hadn't even known I was

missing—freedom to dress, behave, love, and act outside a narrow conventional range. I watched agog as same-sex couples
wandered through the streets in the Castro holding hands and
even kissing. I had seen drag queens in Paris, but they were very
discreet. On the streets of San Francisco, there were men dressed
as women and women dressed as men and every shade of self-
expression in between. I had never seen anything like it.

San Francisco was like a different planet, where there were
no rules about how you needed to be. The liberal vibe seemed
to resonate even at the level of architecture. God knows Paris is
beautiful, but its beauty is tasteful, stately, unchanging, a city
without a hair on its head out of place. The colors of San Francisco, on the other hand, were brilliant and vibrant. A few
months after arriving, I got a tattoo, an artwork on my upper-
left arm depicting a pair of wings, to symbolize a spirit set free.

If the city felt like a gift, it was the attitude of the people that
really took my breath away. I had no job, no credit score, no
connections, and my English was far from perfect. And yet in
those first few weeks, I felt the welcoming energy of the people
in a way I couldn't help but compare to the way foreigners
were treated at home. Whenever I met someone, their attitude
seemed to imply: show me what you've got and I'll give you
what you need, rather than show me your degree certificate and
then we'll talk. In San Francisco, it felt as if it might be possible
to get ahead without having attended the best school or made
all the right decisions since the age of fifteen.

Of course, I was also one of the lucky ones: as an educated, white French person, I represented a category of immigrant that gets a very easy time relative to the vast majority of those who come to the United States. Even my lack of English could play in my favor—the French accent still has its charms—and I knew I was tremendously privileged. There was a big community of French people in the city, many of whom my boyfriend knew and with whom I immediately felt at home, but even without them, I found my feet pretty quickly. Everyone seemed to have come to San Francisco from somewhere else, creating an instant community of strangers. I can be a bit of a loner, but in this city where everyone was an outsider, I found it relatively easy to fit in.

I was lucky for another reason. Within six months of my arrival, my relationship with my boyfriend had ended and I needed somewhere to live. These days, a broke twenty-five-year-old trying to survive in the most expensive rental market in America would not be a happy story. But in the early 1990s, you could still find somewhere charming in San Francisco for relatively little. After trudging around the city looking at listings for days, I found a one-bedroom apartment in Russian Hill and fell for it instantly. It was tiny, with round windows overlooking the Golden Gate Bridge and a rent of $750 a month, considered expensive back then but that these days would barely rent you a windowless shoebox room. I moved in and my real life began.

The first thing I did was apply for a series of jobs as a waitress; it seemed like a good way to learn about the city's food culture. I was surprised by how familiar elements of the food scene in the city were to me. San Francisco was ground zero of the farm-to-table movement, which, after all my years on my grandmother's farm, was something with which I instantly identified. If I ever felt homesick, all I had to do was wander down to the Bay and take a deep breath; the salt in the air and the sight of the unmanicured shore whisked me straight back to the northwest coast of France. A lot of the food in San Francisco seemed to express the city's physical surroundings in a way that reminded me of the food at home.

There were still things I found alien. One of the biggest food shocks was the bread. My god. It wasn't even bread. It was bleached flour, and then slapped around a pile of random ingredients that I barely recognized as a sandwich. I couldn't get my head around American fridges, either, which were three times the size of what I was used to in France and seemed to invite waste. Why buy food in such quantities that half of what you bought ended up being thrown out?

People say the social safety net is better in France, and had I emigrated ten years later, I would have missed living in a country with free health care and all the other benefits. But I had never lived as an adult in France; I had moved straight from my parents' house to a new country where, as far as I was concerned, the way they did things was the way things were. I was young. I was bold. I was excited to be in America. I didn't have health insurance and in those early weeks and months, I didn't care. All I cared about was doing the things I needed to do to be where I wanted to be.

The difficulty for me, as ever, was in deciding what that was. I had turned up in San Francisco without a career plan beyond the desire to get taken on in a kitchen, and I wasn't even 100 percent sure about that. I still knew I loved to cook. But in spite of my dreams of one day owning a restaurant, I had no way of knowing whether, when it really came down to it, I could cut it in a commercial kitchen.

Getting a read on the city's restaurant scene was also proving tricky. If you go to Japan, or Italy, there is a broad uniformity to the culinary culture, through which you can start to understand the story of the country. The same goes for France. Most people have a fixed idea of French cooking that overarches regional differences and boils down to a few totemic dishes and ingredients. It might be a cliché, but through the French love of garlic, bread, and rich sauces, something of the national character shines through.

In America, there is no such homogeneity, and as I hopped between waitressing jobs and tasted my way around San Francisco, I realized this was a city—and a country—with no single story. I had to laugh; after years of resenting the narrowness of the French, now I was bamboozled and a little paralyzed by the sheer scale of American diversity.

After ten months in the city, at least one part of the picture became unexpectedly clearer. After breaking up with my boyfriend, I didn't date for a while. Then one night, at a bar in North Beach where I was waitressing, a large group of women came in. They became regulars and eventually one of them invited me for drinks after my shift. I had seen and been daz-zled by the city's vibrant gay life, but it would never have oc-curred to me to go to a gay bar alone. I don't like crowds and I'm not big into scenes. Besides which, I'd only ever dated men. But that night, when I walked into the gay bar with her, she said: "I think this is where you belong."

I had never felt myself actively to be in denial, so this didn't feel like a thunderclap moment. But it did feel like a shift in perspective. If my friend was right, it would explain certain dis-comforts from my past. Still, it was hard to know in the abstract. I enjoyed myself immensely that night in the bar, but was this really where I belonged? And then I met Melinda.

My parents and I didn't fight a lot when I was a teenager. But there was one subject, however, on which my dad and I repeatedly and explosively clashed, and that was homo-sexuality.

The topic came up in our house only because Philippe, my boyfriend at the time, had a brother who was gay. Philippe, ah Philippe. I wonder where he is now. I met him at a nightclub in Paris just before my eighteenth birthday and he was my first real boyfriend. He was slightly older than me and lived in the 12th arrondissement, in an eclectic building that housed a lot of immigrants. I remember climbing the stairwell to see him and enjoying the smells of all the different kinds of cooking, mostly African, wafting out into the hall.

In conversation one day, I mentioned to my dad that Philippe's brother, Jean-Marie, was gay and had been given a tough time by his family; we should invite him over for Christmas, I said. To my amazement, my dad disapproved. I suppose I shouldn't have been so surprised. Homophobia is still rife in France; according to the Association of Gay and Lesbian Parents, only four same-sex couples have succeeded in adopting in France since 2013. My parents had gone against the Church on so many contentious issues, including abortion and women's rights, but on this one subject—my mother didn't say much, but I knew she agreed with my dad—they were both full-on Catholic traditionalists.

"There's nothing wrong with loving someone of the same sex!" I raged. My dad pushed back. Things got quite heated. When he wouldn't hear me out, I lost my temper—I mean really lost it. "I can't wait for you to die!" I yelled. "I hate you! You can't talk like this!" (Bear in mind I was still only eighteen.) After versions of this fight happened a couple of times, my dad got so annoyed he actually chased me around the dining-room table.

I had no idea I was defending my future self. I simply found my dad's disapproval of Jean-Marie nonsensical. My dad's obstinacy, when he was ordinarily so rational, enraged me.

I could've been kinder; my parent's generation didn't have the education we did and their views on sexuality needed time to evolve. And my dad's prejudices weren't violent. He was a Catholic who, as he saw it, was respecting his religion, but he was never the sort of person to say, "Oh, you're gay, I'm not going to talk to you." I have tried to be understanding about this, not least because my parents were always loving and supportive of me. As lifelong Catholics, they acted within the limitations of their faith and I am grateful for the progress they made. When Jean-Marie came to our house, my dad was cordial, and over the course of a long, fascinating conversation about art and politics found Jean-Marie to be charming and clever. After that, when the topic of homosexuality came up, my dad's tone softened considerably. My mother, who had always been more mildly opposed to it than my dad, followed suit.

Years later, when I took girlfriends home to France, my parents were totally welcoming.

Even for me, getting to a place of complete comfort with my sexuality has been a journey. To some extent, I'm still on it. I think my reticence has less to do with the ripple effect of those early fights about homosexuality with my parents, and more with the fact that I don't like to be boxed into a category. Just as I hate being called a "female chef," I hate being defined by my sexuality. Any label that reduces a person to a single characteristic seems to me designed to diminish them.

After I had been in San Francisco for a year and a half, I moved from Russian Hill to an apartment in an old Victorian house owned by a teacher. It was a studio with a little deck and a Japanese-style interior in which everything was made out of wood. It was tiny and charming and suited me perfectly and it was from here, one balmy night at the end of September, that I set out to meet friends at the Folsom Street Fair.

Since its inception thirty years ago, the Folsom Street Fair has attracted thousands of people to a thirteen-block radius south of Market Street, to celebrate freedom of expression within the gay, leather, and BDSM communities. It is very flamboyant and fun, full of music and dancing and wild fetish gear, and although I was no longer new to San Francisco, I still found it an eye-opener. Looking around the fair that night, I experienced a renewed sense of wonder: these people were all being precisely who they wanted to be.

A friend was performing and I gravitated toward the music area of the festival. It was while I was standing by the stage that I noticed a woman standing a little way from me. She noticed me, too, and for a moment we stared at each other before snapping back to watch the performance. A week or so later, I went out dancing with a friend to a club called The EndUp, and there she was—the woman from the fair.

She looked, I thought, like a combination of Julia Roberts and Cindy Crawford, with very long hair and kind eyes. When we started chatting, I discovered she was a chef working at a fine-dining restaurant in the city and about to open a new restaurant in the Castro. She took my hand and we danced for hours, finally winding up at a twenty-four-hour restaurant called Sparky's. We would be together for the next seven years.

I had noticed Melinda because she was beautiful. But I fell

in love with her because of everything else. She was sweet and well-spoken—a little bit motherly, perhaps. She was confident, and gentle, and she knew San Francisco better than anyone. I had seen the fun side of the city, but when I looked at it again through her eyes, I started to see another side—how it was made up of many marginalized groups, some of them veterans of the city's heyday in the sixties who later had fallen on hard times. Melinda's compassion for these people was inspiring to me, as was the way she looked after her family. Her parents had passed away and she was like a mother to her large brood of siblings, all of whom welcomed me absolutely. As our relationship developed, it started to feel like having a family in the city. It was wonderful.

After six months of dating, we started to look for a place to move in together. I found a little house on Ord Street in Upper Market, and when I turned up to see it, found a mob scene of twenty or thirty other people who also wanted to rent the place. I could see why. It was a two-bedroom, one-bathroom cottage, behind a big Edwardian building, with a garden and a fireplace—totally adorable, and the race was on. I worked every angle I had, hamming up my French accent, playing the little girl from France who had come all this way and only wanted to move in with her girlfriend. The owner listened to my story and what can I tell you? We got the cottage. It felt like a sign from the universe.

Two chefs living together can spell trouble—too much competitive energy—but crucially, I wasn't a chef yet. When I met

Melinda, I had just found my first job in a kitchen and was learning the ropes, while she was a well-established chef, running the kitchen at 2223. We shared an interest in food, of course, but we founded a life together based on our other shared values.

I admired Melinda's professional style, but I admired her kindness more. She really connected with her customers, and as a result 2223 became a beloved neighborhood restaurant, and thirty years later, long after it has closed, is still spoken of fondly in the Castro.

When she set up 2223, it was her aim to make the restaurant like a home away from home. Everyone was made to feel welcome—it wasn't like those fine-dining restaurants where everyone walks around on eggshells. In the Castro, there were a lot of people who had lost their partners in the AIDS crisis. These were single, often quite lonely, older people for whom it was nice to have a place where they could find good food and a warm welcome. Melinda's philosophy was that cooking was about embracing and nurturing, and in every detail her restaurant seemed to imply, Hey, this is my house, my kitchen—and I'm inviting you in.

Six

STARS

J eremiah Tower was the most famous chef in the world, or so it seemed in the early 1990s. After helping Alice Waters put Chez Panisse on the map, he had opened Stars in San Francisco in 1984. By the time I arrived in the city in 1989, it was one of the most talked-about restaurants not only in San Francisco, but in the entire country. Mikhail Gorbachev had eaten there, as had Luciano Pavarotti, Liza Minnelli, Sophia Loren, and Rudolf Nureyev, while Tower himself had become a celebrity.

I had been in San Francisco for a little over eighteen months and hadn't rushed to find work in a kitchen. I had found my feet slowly, meeting people in the restaurant industry, at first through the French community, then through my waitressing. Everyone I met, I asked the same question: who did they think I should work for?

Tower's name kept coming up. He was the best in the business, but it wasn't only that. I had read his memoir and got the sense we were alike. Tower's father had worked in global sales and he had grown up all over the world, combining French, English, and American sensibilities. His culinary style was known to be playful, his personality bold. Tower had studied architecture at Harvard and became a chef in his late twenties, entering his first kitchen with no professional experience. And although he was an admirer of classical French cooking, he was also a believer in the virtue of simplicity.

Something else about Tower appealed to me. While, like most chefs, it was said he could be imperious, I had heard through the grapevine that those who worked for him were given more freedom than in any other kitchen in the city. I liked the idea of working at the epicenter of the new California cuisine, but, more than that, I was attracted to Stars as a restaurant that was as far from the autocratic French kitchen as a chef with no training could get. All I had to do was pluck up the courage to walk in and ask for a job.

It might seem strange that I was even considering this approach, given my lack of professional experience. Apart from that stint making sandwiches for the kids at summer camp in Garches, I had only ever cooked for family and friends. And yet I knew I was good, and not only because my mother had told me. I knew it the way one knows the most profound things about oneself, without need of analysis or explanation. I was so confident, I even thought that "being good" or "not being good" was the wrong way to think about it. It was, I believed, about understanding why you wanted to cook. It was about knowing that when you cook something, even just a sandwich, it's really an act of communication and caring. You can learn cooking techniques, but knowing exactly why you are using them is something you can't always teach. In a funny way, I felt as if I already had the hardest part down.

The restaurant was on Redwood Alley, near City Hall, with a grungy exterior and an entrance via an alley that had a speak-easy vibe. Walking into the kitchen, I recognized Tower immediately from his appearances in the press. He was tall and good-looking, impeccably dressed in chef's whites, and commanding the space with a calm and effortless air.

What happened next still makes me laugh: with the absolute confidence of youth, I walked right up to Tower, looked him straight in the eye, and said, "I want to work for you. I'm French so I already know how to cook." I knew that Tower had pulled a similar move in the early 1970s went he'd marched into Chez Panisse and asked Alice Waters for a job. And I knew from his memoir that he believed in dreams. I had no idea whether hiring people with no experience was something he had a habit of doing, but I had a sense he only wanted to hire people who really wanted to work there.

Tower looked at me for a moment as if sizing me up. Then, instead of throwing me out or asking for references, he said simply, "Okay, come back tomorrow."

I walked out of the restaurant in a state of euphoria. I had done it! I had plucked up the courage to ask, and now I had a shot at the big time! I'd been dreaming of working in a kitchen so long, the fact that it was finally happening felt simultaneously unreal and like a foregone conclusion. I was thrilled, and excited, and determined not to be intimidated. Getting the chance to try out at a restaurant like Stars was precisely the kind of opportunity I'd moved to America for. I wasn't going to ruin it by panicking.

The next day, however, when I returned to the restaurant, my nerves really started to kick in. I looked around the half-empty kitchen. It was early in the day, many hours before the jump and hustle of the predinner rush, but this was scarier in a way than a busy kitchen might have been—the eerie calm before the storm. What if I couldn't take the pace? What if, after all these years of dreaming, I wasn't up to the job? There weren't many women working at Stars, just a few in the pastry division, and as I walked in to report for my shift, I felt a shiver of apprehension. What if there were no women at Stars because, as the entire French culinary establishment had warned me, women couldn't hack it?

To begin, I was put on prep duty. All morning I stood at my station helping prep basic ingredients. I sliced vegetables and peeled potatoes. I washed things and stirred things. "Oui, chef!" I called out, when Jeremiah addressed me, trying to attract as little attention as possible. If I could get through a couple of shifts without messing up, I thought, perhaps they'd allow me to stay.

A few hours before opening, Jeremiah gathered the team for

a meeting. I hovered at the edge of the group, hoping to be either ignored completely or sent down to the basement to peel more potatoes. Instead, Jeremiah turned to me. "Dominique!" he said. I jumped. "Oui, chef!" I said.

"You'll be on the line with Sean tonight." Sean was the sous-chef, the head chef's number two, and on a busy night, the real power in the kitchen. What on earth was going on? I was being taken off grunt work after a single morning and being given a chance to put together some dishes. "Oui, chef!" I said, hoping my voice wasn't trembling.

I looked around the kitchen. There were stations for meat, fish, and pastry. There was the sautéing area, a wood-fire oven and a grill, and there were stations for oysters and hot and cold appetizers. Everything was quiet—it was still early—with the condensed energy of a theater before curtain up. I could barely believe I was here, that I was about to be trusted to put together even the simplest of ingredients for a restaurant so famed and so large. But if my confidence wavered, Sean didn't seem to notice. He turned to me and asked if I'd get going on some couscous. I took a deep breath. Okay, here we go.

The brigade system—le brigade de cuisine—works in French restaurants the way a ranking hierarchy works in the army. It was developed by Auguste Escoffier, the famous French chef of the first part of the twentieth century who, if he didn't exactly invent Hollandaise sauce, was certainly the first to formally codify it. (He definitely invented peach melba.) The way an efficient kitchen should work, he determined, was through a rigid class system that culminated in the chef de cuisine, ran down through the sous-chef, the cuisinier, the commis chef, and so on, and ended with the porter and the pot scrubber. It wasn't impossible for a famous French chef to start out peeling potatoes and rise to the top of the pyramid, but such a move would take decades, during which time he—and it would always be a he—would be expected to obey the orders, and the recipes, of those above him.

This was not how things worked at Stars. There were no recipes, just guidelines. "Make mayonnaise," said Sean and left me to it. "Make mashed potatoes," he said. These were not hard things to make, but when you are helping to plate four or five hundred covers a night, the smallest mistake can feel like a disaster. This is why the brigade system was developed in the first place—to limit the extent to which anyone might lose their head and mess up by denying them the right to make even the tiniest decision. There was a cost to this, however. Inevitably, over the years, the system corrupted into a chain of command so inflexible that those at the bottom were given no opportunity to shine and those at the top grew too fond of power. Kitchens became rife with abusive behavior. It became de rigueur to brutalize one's staff.

I was lucky at Stars. Sean was not the kind of sous-chef who got a kick out of oppressing those lower down on the food chain, nor was he a guy who just wanted to finish his shift and go

My role model, Chef Jeremiah Tower.

home. He was interested in teaching and guiding his staff, a decent human being and a rarity in that role at that time.

I didn't crumble on that first night nor did I panic. Even if I had, however, I wouldn't have been screamed at. Jeremiah's kitchen was not the kind of place where new recruits were put through the culinary equivalent of hazing. There was no yelling, no shouting, no slamming people up against the wall. There was just quiet collaboration and the encouragement to learn.

This is how it should be. Kitchen culture has improved enormously since I started out, and the cliché of the raging chef is less relevant than it once was. But only recently, I interviewed a young guy as a potential sous-chef in my kitchen and was shocked by his attitude. "Yeah," he said, "I worked under this chef in France and got beaten up and yelled at—but I guess if I do that here I might get sued?" He was under thirty.

I was fortunate that my first exposure to a professional kitchen wasn't like that. In Jeremiah's kitchen, if a new recruit showed promise, she was given more responsibility, and within a few weeks I was being presented with a handful of ingredients—calamari, say, and a few herbs and vegetables—and invited to create my own dishes. At 4:30 p.m., Sean, Mark Franz, the executive chef, or Jeremiah would walk over to my station to taste and review. If the dish wasn't working, I would have thirty minutes to fix it. If it worked, it was rolled out in the restaurant that night. There was pressure, of course, but it was managed and orderly. We all looked to Jeremiah, and as long as he wasn't yelling and panicking, neither were we.

I still had moments of doubt. Had I really talked my way into this place on the basis of a French accent and a cocky attitude? It would be a long time before I stopped waiting for someone to call me out across the kitchen—Hey, you! Who let you in!?—and send me home. But even during the most frantic parts of the night, when plates flew and hundreds of people waited for food, I was never paralyzed. The calm of Jeremiah's kitchen gave me the confidence to take a breath and clear my head. I watched and followed. I remained totally focused. I based my performance on three things: observation, intuition, and anticipation, and I sometimes found that my hands worked faster than my brain.

I might not have known exactly what I was doing or why, but my body apparently did. Being a chef is an intensely physical exercise in which muscle memory can play a large part. Mark Franz would later tell me that from the very beginning, I never had to be told something more than once and I never had to redo my dishes. You couldn't, with those guys around. You had to find your feet quickly and then stay on your toes.

I was drawn to food from the earliest age, but I can honestly say that the light didn't really come on until I was in Jeremiah's kitchen. To dream of cooking when you are a kid is one thing; to have this concrete feeling of it being the right thing for you is something else entirely. Being a chef isn't just about being able to cook. It is about being able to think clearly, quickly, and to be good under pressure—to thrive in a challenging environment. You have a dream but it might not fit who you are, and most of us don't know who we are until we grow up. I had always known I loved food, but it wasn't until those early weeks at Stars that I knew with complete conviction and for the first time in my life that I was in the right place.

One thing I noticed about Jeremiah: he liked to leave the kitchen to wander around the dining room, greeting the diners as if they were guests in his home. This seemed to me extremely civilized. If I ever had my own restaurant, I vowed, I would do the same thing.

In addition to Jeremiah, I was fascinated by Loretta Keller, who ran the café at Stars. This was an informal offshoot of the main restaurant, where the food was rustic, delicious, and often made from leftovers from the Stars kitchen—that is, perishable items not used in the kitchen that night that could be reconstituted into dishes the next day. Jeremiah could be whimsical, serving hotdogs, sauerkraut, and champagne at the Stars bar, while at the café, Loretta did something closer to home cooking.

The main thing I admired about Loretta was her attitude toward waste. She was way ahead of the crowd when it came to understanding the implications of industrial food production. Fifty years ago there was almost no waste. Even these days, in France, there is much less food waste than in the United States, where it can be cheaper to buy in bulk and throw away than to buy a lesser amount of what you actually need. This was one of the things that most shocked me when I first came to America—the sheer quantity of food it is apparently okay to throw away. If you looked in my (small, European) fridge today, you would find very little; some butter, some milk, maybe an open jar of tapenade. I buy what I need and no more than that.

Loretta would go on to open Coco500, a hugely influential restaurant (early menu items: stuffed squash blossoms, sautéed scallops with green beans, and quail stuffed with sausage) that closed in 2014 after twenty-three years of being a San Francisco institution. But it was the example she set at the Stars café that stayed with me: the effort to use what in other kitchens might be classified as waste; the simplicity of style.

These were insights that, along with everything else I learned at Stars—how to treat the people who work for you, how to run a calm and compassionate kitchen—set the tone for the rest of my career, as did Jeremiah's generosity to me over the years. He has always been the first to congratulate me when I've had any kind of public recognition, telling me at a Stars reunion recently, when I thanked him for his inspiration, that I was the inspiration now.

But back then, I still had an awful lot to learn. I remember asking Mark Franz in those early days how much it would cost me to start my own restaurant and him replying five hundred thousand dollars. It seemed an impossible figure—where on earth would I ever get that kind of money?—but of course it is completely laughable now. In San Francisco these days, half a million dollars would barely buy you a kitchen.

Sometimes ignorance is necessary in order to move forward. Things had gone so well for me in the first year of my life as a chef, I had become thoroughly convinced of two things: that after my sure start at Stars, I had been able to skip that part of the traditional chef's training in which the novice gets yelled at and abused by her boss; and that it wouldn't be long before I had my own restaurant. On both counts, I was completely, utterly, stratospherically wrong.

*Artwork by Papa Crenn in the dining
room of Atelier Crenn.*

PART TWO

PART TWO

─────────

Seven

MOVING ON

elinda's style of cooking at 2223 was low key and delicious, with an approach that was more rustic than mine. I was starting to discover an interest in experimentation, with a strong desire to fuse flavors from different parts of the world; she was more rooted in Californian cuisine. Our personas in the kitchen were different, too. I kept a calm exterior but a lot of the time ran on nervous energy, where Melinda was more relaxed. When we traveled to France, she met my parents and they quietly approved. "She balances you very well," they said.

After eighteen months at Stars, I was starting to feel restless. I needed to make more money and I needed to broaden my experience. Developing as a chef is entirely dependent on movement, learning what one can from one small kitchen before moving on to the next. One day in 1993, while sitting having a drink at an oyster bar, I ran into the executive chef of the Park Hyatt who, after we got chatting, gave me his card. I called a few days later and he recommended me for a job at a restaurant called Campton Place, near Union Square. I accepted immediately.

On the surface of things, Campton Place did not look like my kind of restaurant at all. It had a white tablecloth dining room with the traditional air of a high-end French restaurant, the type of restaurant I had fled France to avoid. From the outset I sensed it was not a good fit. But—and unusually—I shrugged off my instincts. I told myself I was becoming too comfortable at Stars. I was growing soft and inflexible. Perhaps a spell in a kitchen to which I was less suited was precisely what I needed.

Just as Jeremiah set the tone in the kitchen at Stars, so the executive chef set the tone at Campton Place, and the two kitchens couldn't have been more different. This man was rough talking and abrasive. He shouted and swore at will, in ways that seemed less to do with getting things done and more with his need to demonstrate power. My schedule was from 3:00 to 11:00 p.m., but he forced me, and everyone else on that shift, to come in to work at 10:00 a.m. If anyone complained he slapped them straight down. "You're going to come at three? You're not going to make it."

When a kitchen is run by someone who mistreats his staff, it is a green light for others to follow suit. The sous-chef took his cue from the boss and at first he was just playful, addressing those below him in a lightly mocking way that was annoying but possible to tolerate. Slowly he became more aggressive. He was verbally abusive and recklessly bullied the staff. One night when we were very busy, I was on the grill and the hot oil splashed all over my arms. It was severely painful and when I looked down at my skin, I saw that the burns were deep.

I needed to be relieved from my station. But when I turned to the sous-chef, he snapped my head off, telling me to stop being pathetic and get back to work.

Beyond this incident, the sous-chef also started to become physical. He tried to touch my breasts and made a lot of very sexual remarks. He was a homophobe, and in reference to my sexuality would say, "Oh, come on, I know you also like guys." It made me very uncomfortable. I knew it wasn't right or proper and I should've gone to human resources, but instead I went to the executive chef and said, "This is unacceptable." I told him I didn't feel safe in his kitchen. I don't know what I expected—this was a place where the boys backed one another up—but even so, his attitude shocked me. "This is the way it is and if you don't like it, you can find another job," he said.

I had never had a problem standing up for myself or others. But this was a new experience for me, having a legitimate complaint met with such derision. I was crazy angry. I knew this behavior was wrong, and the worst thing was that the chef didn't care. (I ran into him recently, for the first time since those days, and he was extravagantly nice to me. It was clear he had no idea I might harbor bad feelings.)

This is the problem with sexism in the kitchen: like sexism

everywhere, it is so normalized that half the time the people doing it don't even notice. The culture is so ingrained that when it does happen, it is easy for it to go unacknowledged.

To me, the most obvious way to make things better for women in the kitchen is to encourage more women to become chefs in the first place. Growing up, I couldn't have named a single female chef. Even now, in New York, just 8 percent of Michelin-starred restaurants have female head chefs. (That figure is 20 percent in San Francisco and Chicago, and zero in Washington, DC.) It might seem perverse, in light of this, that I push back about being labeled a "female chef." You can't champion minority rights without naming them first. But in 2016, when the World's 50 Best Restaurants list awarded me the title "World's Best Female Chef," it felt like a double-edged sword. There was no mistaking the implication: that "best female chef" was a lesser category than the one unqualified by gender.

I didn't lose my temper or storm out that day at Campton Place. I simply said okay to the chef, stayed on for a few months while I looked for another job, then left. I had been there for a total of six months, a short time in the scheme of things, but foot-draggingly long when you are having a terrible time. I tried not to let my experiences in an abusive kitchen dent my confidence; I tried to learn from it, to harden my resolve to always trust my own instincts. And I looked with renewed respect at Loretta and Melinda, two women who ran their own restaurants with strength, grace, and dignity. This, I thought, is what should be evoked by the use of the term "female chef," a promotion, not a circumscription, of female excellence. It should never be assumed that the best among us can't go toe to toe with a man.

After Campton Place, I was rattled but determined to get right back into the kitchen. I did a few short-term jobs, one of which was working with Melinda at 2223. This seemed like a brilliant idea when we had it. Spending all day with Melinda in a restaurant I loved and admired would be the ultimate antidote to my experience at Campton Place. I would be safe, and supported, and get to spend all day with the woman I loved. What could possibly go wrong?

It turned out, of course, to be a terrible idea, as couples working together frequently discover. Our styles of cooking didn't easily mesh. And though at home being at different points in our careers had been a virtue, ensuring we weren't in competition with each other, at work it meant Melinda was my boss. It was weird and unsettling for both of us. The biggest problem, however, was that trying to work and live together gave us too little time off from each other, and when a new opportunity arose, I grabbed at it.

I had been working in a professional kitchen for just over three years and was still young and relatively inexperienced. But I was making good connections with senior chefs in the business, and, in 1996, I was offered my first executive chef job. This was huge—a chance to run my own kitchen.

The restaurant, YoYo Bistro, was based at the Miyako Hotel in San Francisco's Japantown. I have always been interested in Japan, both the culture and the cuisine. My dad was fascinated by the samurai, and would tell me stories of their martial prowess and noble sacrifice in battle. From what I'd heard, Japan was similar to France in its strict adherence to tradition, and it was a culture to which I felt intuitively close. But while I always paid attention to the flavors and techniques when I ate Japanese food, I had never visited the country and had no training in cooking in that style.

I was an odd choice, then, to run a Japanese-French fusion restaurant. In the kitchen there would be a Chinese chef, a Korean chef, and running the show, me—a French person. I could have said, No, I'm not qualified for this job, but I loved the idea of combining the cuisines and I was curious and eager. I thought I could do it.

The outgoing chef left a solid menu that I didn't interfere with too much at first. The three of us in the kitchen developed an easy working style. There were so few of us, yelling would have been a ludicrous approach, but in any case it came naturally to me to create an atmosphere of collaboration in which we tried to learn from one another and cook good food.

I don't remember many of the individual dishes I made at Yoyo Bistro, although I know there was a monkfish that went down very well. What I do remember from that period is how I drew on my memories of French cooking and tried to convert them into lighter versions using Japanese ingredients. These were my first steps toward developing my style as a chef, and forming the foundations on which everything would rest. It felt very natural to me to return to my French roots and build up a flavor base from there. In the five years since I'd left France, my frustration with the country had waned, to be replaced with a tentative yearning to revisit it in my cooking, albeit in heavily reconstituted form.

I liked blending, and refining, and paring things down. I started to make a lot of broth. It's such a simple thing, but it took on a huge importance in my mind. I loved the purity and intensity of flavor of broth. I loved the fact that it was nourishing and cleansing at the same time. And I loved its transparency. I didn't want to hide anything.

Yoyo Bistro started to get good reviews. One of them was a three-star review in *Access San Francisco*, an influential annual catalog. And we started to attract a smart crowd. There were celebrities in the restaurant every night at Stars, but I was usually too far back in the kitchen to see them. At Yoyo Bistro I was the boss, and one night in 1996 we were starting to close when the manager received a call and, walking into the kitchen, told me we had to stay open. A party was coming in: it was Juliette Binoche and others coming direct from the premiere of *The English Patient*.

Celebrities can be oblivious to everyone but themselves, and most of the people in the party that night were just that—except for Juliette. Whenever a server approached her, she was gracious and said thank you. After the meal, she came back to the kitchen and thanked my two colleagues and me, as we stood there pouring sweat. I've cooked for a lot of famous politicians and movie stars since then, but Juliette was by far the most cordial.

It was that year that I turned thirty-one. Thirty itself had passed in a blur while I'd been settling in at YoYo Bistro. When a milestone occurs in my life, the feelings attached to it can take a while to turn up, and such was the case here. It took me a year after turning thirty to realize something startling: I wasn't an ingenue anymore. I wasn't the person in my twenties who knew less than everybody else in the kitchen. I knew things, and not only that, I knew people! I was starting to feel like a valued part of the wider chef community. Many of my friends and colleagues in the cooking world were French, people like Roland Passot (La Folie), Hubert Keller (Fleur de Lys), Jean-Pierre Dubray (The Dining Room at the Ritz-Carlton). In France, I had assumed that, as a young woman from a family with no background in cuisine, I would be shut out of these influential networks; in San Francisco, the doors swung wide open.

Six years after starting at Stars, a friend of a friend in the French chef community told me he was involved in reopening a big five-star hotel in Jakarta, at the heart of which would be an $80 million restaurant focusing on Californian-French food. They were looking for a chef who knew both cuisines, he said. Would I be interested?

I was doing well at YoYo Bistro. I loved San Francisco, where other executive chef jobs were sure to be on the horizon. And I was in a relationship with someone who had no intention of leaving California. And yet I found myself wondering about the offer. There was one more intriguing detail about the job in Jakarta; it was, I had been told, the hotel management's desire that, either as a gimmick, an experiment, or a political gesture, the kitchen would be staffed entirely by women.

Eight

INDONESIA

If you had told me ten years earlier, that in the summer of 1997 I would be an executive chef in San Francisco, with the pick of other executive chef posts in the city, I would have laughed and had a tough time believing you. If you had told me that, later that same year, I would have left all of that—along with my relationship of seven years—to move to Indonesia, a country about which I knew nothing and had no prior interest, I would have said you were crazy. It is a mark of ambition never to allow oneself to grow too comfortable, but it is a mark of perversity, too. Clearly I have both in my system.

The culinary scene in San Francisco is broad and vibrant, but still, it is a city of under a million people, and after almost eight years of working in the restaurant industry, I was familiar with all the main players and beginning to feel claustrophobic.

I have never been good at treading water, and I needed a shot of adrenaline.

There was something else going on, too. After seven years together, Melinda and I had slipped into a kind of stasis. For most of my twenties, our time together had been amazingly nourishing, a relationship of mutual support and encouragement. Melinda had opened up the city for me, provided me with a family away from home, and showed me, through her example, that being a great chef was bound up with the integrity of one's personal relationships. But while I would go on admiring her, it felt as if our relationship had reached a natural conclusion. Endings can be difficult to spot when they happen, and for a while Melinda and I had been ignoring the signs. There was no drama. We weren't fighting. But I needed to move on, and maybe moving countries was the cleanest and easiest way to do it.

All things being equal, Jakarta would not have been my first choice. While there were many parts of the world—Spain, Japan, the Middle East—I had long been obsessed with, Indonesia wasn't on my radar at all. I had no idea what the food scene there was like, but I knew there would be very specific challenges. The reason a female-only kitchen was considered exciting and risqué in the first place was because women in Indonesia in that era had relatively few professional opportunities and little visibility in positions of prominence. If I took the job at the InterContinental Hotel, I would be the first female executive chef in the country. The opportunity to do good and inspire other women was compelling, but to be the first to do anything is to invite high levels of scrutiny and, more often than not, hostility, too. I wondered if there'd be a backlash or if I was being set up to fail.

Chefs are freelancers; they have little or no long-term security. The closest we can come to enjoying the trappings of a regular job, with pension contributions, paid leave, and good promotion prospects, is to get taken on by one of the large hotel chains, and after changing jobs for eight years, that was definitely part of the appeal. The InterContinental, like the Park Hyatt, is a highly sought-after employer and a safe way, I thought, to broaden my horizons and see a bit more of the world. And so I did something unwise: I suppressed my reservations in favor of the security blanket of a big corporate employer. At the planning stage, everything seemed wonderful and exactly as I hoped it would be. When you move across the world with a luxury hotel chain, the logistics are made very easy. You don't have to find lodging; you simply live in the hotel. All the facilities, from housekeeping to the tennis courts to room service and the pool, are at your disposal. I had seen a photo of the hotel and it looked like a palace surrounded by a fabulous garden. In my wilder imaginings, I pictured myself on the equivalent of an extended five-star working vacation, a million miles from my modest life in San Francisco.

There was one odd detail: the hotel itself, although run by the InterContinental group, was owned by the family of Suharto, the military dictator who had been in power in Indonesia since 1967.

This should have rung alarm bells. But by the time I came across this detail, I had made up my mind that I was leaving. I continued to ignore my doubts and pressed on with my plans.

Since arriving in America nine years earlier, I had become superstitious about first impressions. Landing in San Francisco for the first time, my overwhelming sense of comfort and recognition had been borne out by the life I came to live in the city. I would feel a similar sense of familiarity when I landed in Tokyo thirty years later.

But the moment I landed in Jakarta, I wanted to get out. I didn't connect. It was hot and chaotic and there was no one from the hotel to meet me. I dragged my suitcase across the concourse, got into a cab, and directed the driver to the Inter-Continental Hotel. As I looked through the window while the unfamiliar scenery sped by, I wondered if I'd made a huge mistake.

The loneliness of those early weeks in Jakarta was difficult. Every night, I sat alone in my one-bedroom suite, surrounded by the empty corridors of the five-star hotel. I didn't have easy access to email and the time difference made phoning home difficult. I knew no one in the city and felt like a virtual prisoner of the hotel compound. In the mornings I would get up and play tennis in the sports complex. I would take long runs through the garden and swim in the pool. To socialize, I would hang out with the general manager in his apartment. But it was an odd, dreamlike time, dislocated from any sense of the wider community.

What saved me was work. I had a kitchen to set up from scratch, and while cloistered in the five-star hotel I had no real chance to connect with the country, connecting with the people was different. The moment I started interviewing women for positions in the kitchen, everything changed for the better.

It is fascinating to me how, across vast divides of language, history, politics, and religion, broad human reflexes can remain the same. Some of these are good, some bad, but of all the universals I've encountered, one of the most depressing to me is the way women internalize lack of opportunity as an expression of their own shortcomings. I was starting to meet and interview young women interested in getting jobs in my kitchen, and the common narrative was the same every time. When I asked a young woman why she wanted the job, she might say, "This is my passion," before adding hesitantly, "but how can I do it when I have no experience? What if I fail? I'm not qualified for the job you are offering."

I would tell them my own story of turning up at Stars with no experience and asking for a job, but they would shake their heads and say that in Jakarta women were always in the back of the kitchen, peeling potatoes and missing out on the action.

I understood this, of course. And I had sympathy. For women, the landscape in Indonesia was different from that of the United States (although let's face it, not that different). But I was also there to create opportunity and to teach them you have to reach out and grab things. At some point I just exploded. "Just fucking do it!" I said. "You guys can do it! We can do it together. Let's be inspired by one another." It was as big a deal for me as it was for them. For my staff, it was a big deal finally to have a mentor who would tell them yes, they could do this thing they had always wanted to do, and for me, it was a big deal to be able to pass on some of the opportunities I had been given myself, and to inspire confidence in women younger than me.

I hired thirteen women in all, all of them Indonesian or Chinese Indonesian. There could have been tension between those two groups. Historically, Chinese Indonesians have been targeted as a minority ethnic group in Indonesia, subjected to discriminatory laws and frequently scapegoated and attacked during periods of political instability. During those first few weeks, I was anxious that these undercurrents would take hold in the kitchen and destabilize the group. Nothing of the sort happened. We were united by the thrill of being together and taking part in what felt like a unique and unprecedented experiment.

I had left San Francisco in a state of near burnout, after working full pelt for eight years. At the same time, the speed with which I had risen through the lower ranks of kitchen life had perhaps made me a little smug. If I had left the city, in part, to fix this attitude before it hardened into complacency, the kitchen in Jakarta and the eagerness of the women I'd hired was like a shot in the arm. During those early days, one young woman I'd hired shyly approached me to say she had dreamed all her life of working in a kitchen, and assumed in Indonesia it would never be possible. I felt immensely humbled.

The menu I developed was Californian-French with a few

Italian undertones. This meant using as many fresh local ingredients as possible, as per the basis of California cuisine. Not only was this hard in Jakarta, it was hard in the context of a hotel kitchen. This is something that would happen again and again in my career—being hired for my creativity, then discovering that the management of the restaurant had no real appetite for change and only liked the *idea* of doing things differently.

The first problem with using local ingredients was one of refrigeration. Deliveries came into the kitchen every morning at 5:00 a.m., an early start made necessary by the fact that it would get very hot later in the day, well into the nineties. But even with deliveries coming in that early, it was still vital to refrigerate en route, and this was difficult if not impossible to organize. There was no infrastructure in the city for refrigerated delivery, which ruled out buying local chicken or fish. Everything was set up to source ingredients from the outside, at vast expense, so that while local markets suffered, the French, German, and Australian import companies made enormous amounts of money.

This wasn't purely a question of logistics. There was a moral dimension, too. Working for a five-star hotel in a developing country is a shocking tutorial in double-standards. Everything I saw in Indonesia was skewed toward pampering the expat at the expense of the local. The very word "luxury" had come to mean foreign bought and imported, rather than anything originating in Indonesia. Locally sourced produce was, by definition, instantly despised as inferior, so that quite apart from my difficulties with refrigerated delivery, when I tried to buy local, it shocked the hotel management—although they never out-right prohibited me from doing it.

As soon as we opened, we were the talk of the town. An all-female kitchen in Jakarta really was a freak show. Every lunch and dinner seating, groups of people—mainly businessmen—came in to gawk at us while eating. A hotel is a strange environment to live in to begin with, but this made it feel even more surreal.

In spite of all this, there were many days of complete happiness. Although the hotel management urged me to source my ingredients from abroad, they didn't try to influence the menu and, within the constraints of the system, I had a lot of freedom. And building my team of thirteen women was like building a community, with a sense of sisterhood that I loved. Our team worked fantastically well together and it was an inclusive and diverse kitchen—at least in racial and economic terms.

In terms of gender, of course, it was single sex, something that in other contexts I have criticized. I don't believe in separating women into their own unique category, but I do understand the value of symbolism. In a country in which women had had so little opportunity, the strength of this particular gesture was self-evident. It was a statement and it worked. People took note. If a hotel chain as prominent as the InterContinental saw fit to hire women chefs, perhaps they weren't so bad after all. And in the context of the InterContinental Hotel in Jakarta, helping to bring about this shift in thinking was deeply gratifying.

After weeks of building up the restaurant infrastructure, training staff, and putting the menu together, I wanted to take my team out to dinner to thank them, and made a reservation at the Park Hyatt, another luxury hotel where the restaurant was supposed to be good. The manager took my name over the phone and a few days later we arrived en masse at the check-in desk at the restaurant. The manager looked at me, looked over my shoulder at my team, and said, "Are you eating with those people?"

Indonesia was a country in transition at that time, as Indonesians fought to free themselves from thirty years of Suharto's rule. My strong sense was that foreigners needed to step aside and let the people of the country lead, but there was still an awful lot of racism to overcome. "Yes, they're my team," I said to the manager of the Park Hyatt. "I made a reservation." And he said, "They're Indonesian."

I was instantly, incandescently furious. The notion that they shouldn't be there was crazy to me, although it was familiar to the rest of my team. One woman leaned in and said to me quietly, "Chef, it's okay, we can go somewhere else." Well, you can imagine. I have never been good at biting my tongue and I have a physical aversion to bullies. "No way," I said and turned to the manager. "Listen: you're going to treat them as well as you're treating me. They're the people of this country, working their asses off, and they deserve to be treated with respect." Reluctantly, he sat us down.

I think of the women I worked with in Jakarta often. To my immense joy, I still occasionally hear from them. I had an email recently from a woman who asked, "Do you remember me?" She had entered my kitchen as a young woman with no experience, and was writing to tell me she was now an executive chef. "You inspired me," she said, "when I thought that path would never be open to me." I replied that of course I remembered her. I said the best experience of my life was being able to inspire and to be inspired by the people around me. "I'm so proud of you," I wrote. "Please continue your success and keep in touch."

That dinner was the first and last time we all went out together. Toward the end of 1997, spurred on by the Asian financial crisis, the Suharto regime started to crumble. Student demonstrations and anti-Suharto riots in Jakarta spread across the country. As the government disintegrated, we spent Christmas holed up in the hotel. It was a particularly unsafe location since it was owned by the Suhartos. None of us was allowed to go out, and expats were told it would be necessary to leave. My contract had been for two years and I sometimes wonder if, had it not been for the riots that Christmas, I would have stuck it out to the end of my term. In spite of the success of the kitchen and my enjoyment of the staff, I was still feeling terribly lonely. I never did connect with the country. And the fourteen-hour time difference with San Francisco felt like an unbridgeable gap.

INDONESIA

When management asked us where, precisely, each of us would like to be evacuated to, I replied without hesitation. "Take me to LA," I said. In spring 1998, Suharto would resign after thirty-one years as president, and I would be back in America.

Nine

LA

A s a kid, all my favorite TV shows were set in LA, from which I gathered it was as far from a sleepy French town as a girl with ambition could get. In LA, people flashed their white teeth in the sun. They jumped into dune buggies and flew across the beach by the ocean. They chased stolen cars down something called the Pacific Coast Highway. Going back to San Francisco so soon after leaving would have felt like an anticlimax, and the prospect of moving to LA seemed wildly exciting.

In the late 1990s, LA wasn't being celebrated for its food culture. This isn't to say the food scene wasn't interesting, particularly with the rise in popularity of Japanese food and the strong Mexican influence in the city. But it wasn't considered a destination for food. The stereotype of the average Angelino is someone too busy trying to stay thin to eat out with any conviction. To me, however, the health consciousness of the city was a bonus. Surrounded by rich agricultural lands and blessed with dry, year-round sunshine, LA sounded like a chef's dream.

Chefs are as subject to trends as anyone, but professional cuisine as a whole can be very intolerant of new tastes, particularly when they are imposed from the outside. When I was growing up in France, even vegetarianism was considered dangerously radical. You didn't ask for sauce on the side, or for lactose-free milk, and no one would have dared call themselves gluten intolerant. To some chefs, the rise in these sensitivities, along with general changes in palates and appetites, has been an unwelcome interference in the kitchen.

I tend not to think like this. Even by the health-conscious standards of San Francisco cuisine, my restaurant has one of the most vegan menus in the city. This is a natural reflection of my interest in plant-based cooking, but it is also a reflection of the times. It has always struck me as bizarre when a chef gets angry when asked to accommodate someone's dietary needs. I make my own decisions in the kitchen and the final say is with me, but I also like to consider the other point of view. I want to welcome people to my house, I don't want to make them feel bad. So you want the sauce without dairy or sugar? Okay! Let me see what I can do. It can be a challenge, but whatever the demand, be it vegan, gluten-free, or fructose-free cooking, I try to meet people's needs.

I'm even relaxed about food being sent back to the kitchen. It rarely happens, but perhaps a dish proves too salty for someone's palate, or isn't cooked enough for their tastes. I try to deal with that respectfully; after all, every palate is different. I happen to like acidity and salt, and I like my fish lightly cooked if at all. But if you come to my restaurant and want everything cooked medium well? Bien sur, I will try to accommodate your terrible taste.

The only thing that really irritates me in the restaurant is when people say, "It's not to my liking." I'm doing a seafood and vegetable menu and occasionally people ask, "Can I have meat?" And I say no; that I don't accommodate. You shouldn't eat here. Or someone says I don't think I like mushrooms, or fish. I am not interested in that. You go out in order to experience new things; there has to be some give and take on both sides.

T he first time I visited LA, I was with my boyfriend Philippe and we were both still in college. When we checked into the YMCA in Hollywood, we found a drab, squalid place nothing like the shining city of my dreams. We immediately checked out, and for the rest of the vacation Philippe and I rented a small bungalow on the water in Malibu.

I loved the ocean and the weather, but the city itself had seemed bizarre. How did it even function as a city? It was so spread out that the definition seemed barely to qualify. And how on earth were you supposed to get around the place without sitting on the freeway for hours every day? When I returned fifteen years later, I don't know if the city had changed or only

I had, but after the stress and disappointment of my time in Indonesia, LA seemed like a balm. For a few months, I stayed in a hotel in West Hollywood, then I found a little duplex in Larchmont. A new life began.

To find a job in LA, I reconnected with my old chef network in San Francisco. YoYo Bistro was situated in a hotel owned by the Radisson group, and it was through one of my hotel acquaintances that I found a position in LA. For a few months, I ran the kitchen at the Radisson in LA's Koreatown, a good entry into the city's culinary scene and one that chimed with my interest in Asian flavors. After my experiences in Indonesia, however, I wasn't ready to commit long-term to working for a big hotel chain, and when a friend heard of a job going at the Manhattan Country Club in the southernmost part of the city, I headed down to take a look.

Manhattan Beach is a thirty-five-minute drive from central Los Angeles, slightly to the south of Marina del Rey. The venue was owned by a man called Keith Brackpool, a British American entrepreneur who was well-connected politically, and the club was known as a destination for visiting politicians. It was quite a spread: 75,000 square feet of land, including 18 tennis courts, a 6,000-square-foot gym, and a 25-meter swimming pool, all of which would sell in 2017 for $73 million. At the center of this was the club restaurant, which I would end up running for almost eight years.

Running the kitchen of the Manhattan Country Club was not like running a fashionable fine-dining restaurant. Despite

Early days at Manhattan Country Club.

the prestige of the venue, compared to Stars, or YoYo Bistro, or even the InterContinental Hotel, it was a laid-back environment. The food had to be good, but there was no pressure to turn it into a traditional fine-dining establishment. It was a sports and social club. Everyone was encouraged to relax.

It was exactly what I needed at that point in my life. After the frantic pace of life in San Francisco, the split with Melinda, and the move to Jakarta and back, what I needed was a few years to kick back in the sun. There were fifteen hundred or so members at the Country Club, and in addition to the daily lunch and dinner menus, Keith engaged me to do a lot of private parties. I cooked for Al Gore. I designed the menu for a big tennis tournament. For these events, I could devise whatever menu I liked. I started to take my time and develop my style.

After I took over the kitchen, the first thing I did was reach out to the farmer communities around LA in order to learn more about the organic movement. I wasn't interested in working with the big food corporations, and preferred to go out and visit small farms and small suppliers, and try to source the best ingredients for the simplest meals. Keith trusted me, and because of that I was able to experiment a lot, and I wasn't made to strictly adhere to recipes.

Cooking this way isn't for everyone. In the early days, before I had much of a reputation to go on, it was hard to attract collaborators who understood what I was doing. One day in the early 2000s, I met with a young man named Juan Contreras. He had heard of me through the grapevine and emailed to ask

Working, cooking, learning.

for a meeting. I hadn't jumped at the chance. I was busy and I had no idea who he was. He emailed again, and again. Juan is quiet and dogged in ways that complement my own dogged-ness, but with a flair for planning I completely lack.

He is also an extraordinarily good chef, although I didn't know it back then. When he walked in the door, I saw a young guy with cutoff pants and sun-bleached hair who looked like a typical Californian surfer. Juan was born in San Diego and is of Mexican descent. His grandfather was a carpenter, his father was a doctor, and his mother, who he had been very close to and who had died when he was young, had been a teacher. We talked for hours at that first meeting, about his life, his dreams, and the loss of his mother. What's interesting is that we didn't talk exclusively, or even overly, about food, yet I immediately had a deep sense of compatibility with him.

(A friend of mine recently asked Juan to recall his first impressions on meeting me. "Crazy!" he said. "All over the place! A lot of ideas and goals!" I guess my energy had yet to find its true focus, although I was many years into planning my own restaurant. "Her strength is in risk-taking. She pulls the trigger and the rest of us go along for the ride.")

In late 2006, I woke up one day and realized I had been at the Country Club for almost eight years. Though I was happy there, the longer I stayed the more remote some of my ambitions seemed to become. It was a good life and a satisfying job, and I was close to the owner. I still am. In many ways, I had gone much further in my career than I could have ever imagined, working in prestigious restaurants and for the biggest names in the business. But in one very specific goal I had fallen short. I had turned forty a year earlier and was starting to panic that if I wanted to open a restaurant, I'd better get on with it.

This goal was about more than being my own boss. From my chef-owner friends, I knew that owning a restaurant was a huge headache. It was financially risky and emotionally fraught and the probability was it would fail. But the reward, if it worked out, was something I could barely imagine. Even at the Country Club, where I had so much freedom, there was a limit to how much influence I could exert. Its look and ethos had been established long before I'd arrived and reflected the owner, not me. I wanted to create something of my own.

Later that year, toward the end of 2006, a pair of restaurateurs approached me and said they were opening a restaurant in Santa Monica. Would I come in with them, as a coinvestor and the executive chef? On the face of it, it seemed a good fit. They talked about farm to table, and organic and local food movements, and they talked about a love of innovation and modernity.

The restaurant was to be called Abode, in a building on Ocean Avenue, across the street from the entrance to the Santa Monica Pier. The interiors were to be warm, with a lot of exposed wood and soft lighting. The menu was to be fresh, seasonal, and wherever possible sourced from farmers using sustainable practices. I would have creative control of the kitchen and a say in the major decisions concerning the restaurant. The most important of these was the staff. Although it had been a couple of years since we'd met, the first thing I did was call Juan. I knew I wanted to work with him and that he would understand my vision instantly. Looking back, it is safe to say that the only good thing to come out of Abode was the beginning of my working relationship with Juan.

There were a lot of things wrong with Abode. The management was chaotic. There was discord over how high end they wanted the restaurant to be and what crowd we were trying to attract. Though we raised over $2 million from investors, most of it, as far as I could tell, was spent on the decor.

I built on many of the recipes I'd devised over eight years at the Country Club and reconfigured them for the new setting. I concocted a lot of small plates, including a pear-and-parsnip "cappuccino" soup, with truffles and coffee on the side. I created an eight-course vegetarian tasting menu as well as a slow-cooked osso buco in apple cider.

We had some good reviews, and a couple of terrible ones. The *Los Angeles Times* complained about the cost of the beef and that too much time had been spent on how the food looked. (The creation of foam, in particular, sent one critic over the edge. "Arts and crafts," she called it.) Nonetheless, the restaurant was runner-up in the 2007 Angeleno's Restaurant Awards, and that same year, *Esquire* magazine named me a "chef to watch." This was a big deal. After working nonstop as a chef for almost fifteen years, I felt I was finally being publicly recognized.

None of these achievements were acknowledged by the people who'd hired me; all I heard from management were complaints. They were cheap, wanting me to work seven days a week without adequate time off, and they were manipulative—

smiling to my face and being rude about me behind my back, which of course I found out about later. I didn't feel I could trust them, nor that they were on my side. The restaurant had barely opened before I was planning my escape.

This is often the downside to being impulsive. I should have done my due diligence before accepting the job. But now that I knew I was in trouble, I was at least decisive about what I needed to do. I find moving on easy, an instinct that is built into my very foundations and probably goes back to my being adopted. Fresh starts, however unscheduled, always energize me, and so after only six months, I left Abode. Six months after that, the restaurant shut. I'd lost the money I'd invested and I had no job, but I didn't care; I was free.

The lesson of all this is that it's never just about the plate. You can have the greatest idea in the world, but if you don't have the right people around you, it will never come to fruition. I didn't have the right people at Abode, so I did what I needed to do to dig myself out, at considerable cost. But the alternative— to shrug and make do; to work with people who didn't look after their staff—was unacceptable to me. I would rather go out of business than do business with them.

Leaving takes stamina. So does standing up for yourself. Even the baseline energy required to run a kitchen day in, day out, is phenomenal, and it's no coincidence that substance abuse is rife in culinary culture. I worked insanely hard in LA in my thirties, but I never had those problems. When people ask how I have so much energy, I tell them the truth: I don't do drugs, I don't drink much alcohol—wine, that's it—and I get exhausted, like anyone else. What drives me is doing things right.

It always has, from the time I first listened to my dad talk about the world over dinner or watched him taking pains over his paintings in the garden. He taught me that success can't always be measured in wealth and acclaim but rather in the satisfaction of doing things right.

However, if I'm to be entirely honest and tell this story right, I have to acknowledge there was something else going on. I worked radioactively hard in my twenties and thirties because I was pursuing a goal and a vision, but that wasn't my only motivation. For the previous eight years, I'd been trying to block something out, something that I would continue to put off thinking about. I didn't want to think about my dad, or the fact that I had lost him.

Ten

PAPA CRENN

There is a photo of my dad as a young man, taken in Marseilles shortly after the war. He is standing alongside Charles de Gaulle at the First Congress of the RPF—the Rassemblement du Peuple Français—the political party de Gaulle founded in 1947 and that for a while drew my father's support. Later, my dad would disagree with much of what de Gaulle stood for politically—he was far too right wing for my dad's politics—and would even participate in the demonstrations against him in Paris in 1968. But he always revered him for his bravery during the war and I think they recognized that trait in each other. When, after the war, de Gaulle rewarded heroes of the Resistance with the title Compagnons de la Liberation, one of them was my dad.

I often think of that photo. A copy of it is held, along with forty-odd other photos of him, in the archives of the Resistance in France. It's all there in black and white: records of my dad's sabotage operations when he was still a teenager, his military training with the American Ninth Air Force and subsequent service as a paratrooper, his contribution to the rebuilding efforts after the war. When he told us the stories, his tone was matter-of-fact and the moral unchanging. Heroism, he said, wasn't a question of movie-like daring. More often than not, it was simply a case of going on.

It was my mother who rang me to tell me that after a period of feeling unwell, my dad had been rediagnosed with prostate cancer. The first diagnosis had been made three years earlier, and now it had come back and spread to his bones. I was gearing up for the move to Indonesia, and my mother's instinct, I realized later, was to downplay things to protect me from worry. I got my dad on the phone, and he also reassured me there was no immediate emergency. He sounded the same as he always had. He and I even talked about death, as we had talked about everything all of my life. He said he wasn't afraid.

I wasn't afraid, either. My dad was invincible, everyone knew that. And the fact that he was able to talk about death somehow made the possibility of it seem more remote. As I managed the difficulties of my job in Jakarta and then set about establishing a new life in LA, I had no real sense of what was happening. But throughout 1998 and into the beginning of 1999, my dad's health steeply declined.

It's a natural parental instinct to protect one's children from harm, and my mother thought she was doing the right thing.

My two men, 1998.

The disease was progressing, but I had just started my new job at the Manhattan Country Club, and in her eyes I was horrendously busy and didn't need the added worry of wondering whether I should be bolting back to France. But I wasn't a child; I was a woman in my thirties and I needed the information. It was later that year, on a hot summer day, that I spoke to my dad on the phone without fully realizing we were so close to the end. He told me that he loved me.

The next time I spoke to anyone from my family, it was my brother, calling with the news. I couldn't understand what he was saying. I simply couldn't process the information. My father was dead, he said, but how could that be? Outside my window, everything looked just the same. But here was this person on the line telling me the entire world had been turned on its head.

I remember nothing beyond the numbness of that day, and in the days that followed, my mind circled around irrelevant details. It was July and, absurdly, what I remember about flying from LA to Paris is that on such short notice the flights were hideously expensive. I changed planes in Paris, taking a small regional flight to Brest, in Brittany, where my brother picked me up. I was wearing summery shorts and a shirt and my brother took one look at me and said you need to change. "Change for what?" I said. He stared at me. "There are people at the house," he replied.

Traffic. I remember that. So many cars parked outside. They went all the way up the street. I entered the house, hugged my maman and other members of the family, then walked slowly up the stairs. In my parents' bedroom my dad was laid out on the bed. I stared at his face, trying to catch a moment of movement. The Catholics believe in the afterlife and I found myself thinking, So where is he now? I wondered if I needed to start believing in God, just so I could believe that my dad wasn't gone. As I stared at his face, the size of my want was so huge that for a split second I was convinced I saw him smile. I lay down next to him and started to cry.

My dad was seventy-four when he died and I was not a child. I had had him for over thirty years, much longer than many people have their parents. And he and I had had the best possible relationship. There was nothing I wished I had told him, no conversations un-had, no I love you's unsaid. But at the end of the day, none of that matters. When you lose someone you love to the extent I loved my dad, no amount of time will ever be enough. I still wanted more.

Eventually, after lying next to my dad for I don't know how long, I forced myself up and returned downstairs. My maman was hosting the mourners, organizing and holding everyone together. She was so strong and I wanted to be strong, too, but at that point I felt completely obliterated. I hadn't eaten since receiving the phone call from my brother almost forty-eight hours earlier. That afternoon, at the funeral, I fainted during the church service.

It would be many, many years before I could process my father's death. In the meantime I worked like crazy.

This sounds like a textbook case of denial, but it wasn't quite that. People in denial live their lives in a clenched, troubled way. But while I worked very hard after my dad's death, setting up the Country Club kitchen and settling into life in LA, I let myself feel the pain of his absence. It was incomprehensible to me, but I still knew he was gone. It was coming to terms with it that took so much time.

When I create something, I oscillate between celebrating the transitory nature of time and trying to figure out how to hold on to it—how to make something fleeting so forceful it stays in one's mind. Mostly I do this through food, but occasionally I try other types of expression. Over time, I would find larger ways to pay tribute to my dad, culminating in the opening of a restaurant that bore his name. Immediately after his death, however, the only way I could find to express my love for him was to write it in a poem.

Papa Crenn,

Sitting on top of the dune, feeling of beach sand under my toes,
Looking so far at the blue sea . . . the sun beaming fiercely on my
Raw heart. I remember we used to sit here together during those
Memorable summer days, listening to your stories and laughing at
Your jokes. Those hot summer days I would hear the echoes of
The fireworks in the sky,

Scarlet buttons . . .
Golden lozenges . . .
Green . . . yellow . . . red . . .

Sweat on my face are the tears of my bruises that you imprint
When you left me. They are not scars but signals of just how far I
Have been and how far I will go . . . with you at my side.

I miss you.
Your daughter

A copy of this poem hangs on the wall of the dining room at Atelier Crenn. I pass it every time I walk from the kitchen to the bar. My life changed when my dad died, and one small effect that persists is that whenever I see a number from France on my phone, my heart freezes. I will never forget the experience of my brother calling me that day. I'm painfully aware that, given my mother is eighty-five, at some point it will happen again.

My dad's death made me reexamine my priorities. It reminded me of how lucky I'd been with my adoption and also made me reconsider what I wanted to do with that luck. I was thirty-four and had already spent years cooking food that didn't really matter to me, and so in those years after my dad's death, I became more resolved than ever that one day I would work for myself. It was my father, after all, who had taught me to always keep going.

My dad died in 1999. Almost twenty years later, I was the subject of a profile on the Netflix show *Chef's Table*, during the course of which cameras followed me back to Locronon. I knocked on the door of my parents' old house in the village, from which they had long since moved on. I walked along the shore where, as a child, I had spent so many happy hours with my family. And I walked around the graveyard where my dad is buried.

It was a strange pilgrimage, not least because I was being followed everywhere by cameras. But as an exercise, it was useful to look back on my life and realize, for what felt like the first time, that I was really at peace with his death. As I spoke of my dad to the interviewer, I understood that I had tried to absorb as much of his life into my own, and that after almost two decades without him, I had arrived at a place where I could let go and embrace who he was.

My dad loved soup. He loved jazz music. He loved his kids and he loved my maman. He taught me how to look at the world in a rare and courageous way and he enabled my adventures, even when they took me away from him. Every year, he loved to wake us at 4:00 a.m. on the first day of the summer and embark on the long drive to Brittany, the place he loved more than anywhere else.

Before I was born, my dad was the deputy mayor of a little village called Pont-Aven in Brittany. It would never have been heard of outside the region were it not for its illustrious association with artists. Paul Gauguin spent his summers in Pont-Aven in the 1880s and set up an artists' colony called the Pont-Aven School, to which such postimpressionist luminaries as Émile Bernard and Armand Séguin belonged. It was here, as a young man, that my father first picked up a brush.

I have an image of him in my head, sitting still for hours in the atelier behind our summer house, intently focusing on his painting. "It was all a question of perspective," he said, "in art as in life." When he took me to a gallery, he would stand me before a particular painting and ask me what I felt. At first, I thought this was a test and I would stand in silence, staring at the painting while desperately searching for the right answer.

Art by Papa Crenn, hanging in Atelier Crenn's dining room.

Eventually, my father told me there was no right answer. "I can't tell you what to think about this painting," he would say. "Because there's no way for any two people to look at a painting the same way. All the artist can do is to create in a way in which we are made to feel *something*. What we feel, what we take away from it, is up to us."

It was the same principle he applied to looking at the world; one could choose how one wanted to see it. For my father, the world was bountiful with gifts, and this is how I came to see it, too. On our annual trip to the coast, we would take long walks on the beach, looking at the birds and gulping sea air. Now and then, my dad would pause to point out some detail of the coastline, where the salt water had carved crescents into the rock. I followed his gaze, and what I saw, of course, had a different perspective. I saw not only what he saw—the sea and the sky—but I saw my dad, too.

Now, when I walk along the shoreline in San Francisco or return home to Brittany, all I have to do to find my dad is look out to sea or up at the sky. He died on the night of Bastille Day, the French national day, when fireworks light up the dark. That night, as my maman came into his room to check on him and kiss him goodnight, he told her, "Soon, there will be another firework in the sky." When she looked in on him in the morning, he was gone.

Papa Crenn.

Sitting on top of the dune, feeling of beach sand
under my toes, looking so far at the blue sea... the sun
beaming fiercely on my raw heart. I remember w...
used to sit here together during those memorable
summer days listening to your stories and laughing a
our jokes. Those hot summer days, I would hear the
echoes of th' fireworks in the sky,
            scarlet buttons......
            golden lozenges...
            green.. yellow.. red...

Sweat on my face are the tears of my
bruises that you imprint when you
left me, they are not scars but signals
of just how far I have been

For Papa Crenn.

Eleven

THE PHONE CALL

In 2004, I was well settled in LA and happily employed at the Manhattan Country Club. Five years had passed since my dad's death, and in 2001 I had bought a tiny bungalow on Raleigh Street in LA, two blocks from what used to be Paramount Studios. In the 1920s, the bungalow and others like it had been built on the studio lot as offices for writers. I redid everything inside and turned it into a tiny, cool base from which to commute daily to the restaurant.

I felt that my life was on a solid enough footing to make a decision that might change everything—to apply for my adoption file and find out the name of my birth mother.

France and Italy are among the small number of countries in which a woman is permitted to give birth "in secret." This means that, after the baby is born and taken away for adoption, the mother's name can be redacted from the birth certificate. In

France, being born in these circumstance is known as being a child né sous X, and such a child will, in all likelihood, never be able to trace his birth parents. He may not even be able to find out their names. My brother was one such child né sous X, and even if he wanted to find out more about the woman who bore him—which he has never shown the slightest inclination to do—such a task would be impossible.

My circumstances were different. Growing up, my parents knew very little of my birth mother, but this wasn't because the information didn't exist. It was because under French law at the time an adoptee's records were sealed. This was in line with the overall thinking in those days that the less an adopted child knew of her origins, the easier her integration with a new family might be. As a child, I had been curious about my birth mother, and my feelings of being set apart from my peers were almost certainly linked to questions around my adoption. But knowing more was never something I obsessed about. I told myself I knew who I was and that was all there was to it.

In 2002, the French government responded to pressure from adoption advocacy groups and altered the law. I couldn't ignore it. I had spent my whole life convincing myself the gaps in my knowledge didn't matter, but there is a difference between being comfortable not knowing something because it can't be known, and deciding not to pursue information when it is readily available.

Along with every other adult adoptee in France, I would be able to apply for my adoption file. Being adopted is a complicated thing. There are always reminders, sometimes even within your own family. My dad's sister, Aunt Josephine, had always been kind to me. She was a doctor who had emigrated from France to Johannesburg while still a young woman and lived there for the next fifty years. She would send my brother and me gifts and was very nice to us when she came to visit. When I lived in Indonesia, she asked me to write to her and wrote me back long, affectionate letters. She was very supportive and had a great deal of respect for my dad.

Aunt Josephine never married or had children. In France, when someone with no immediate family dies, it's customary for a surviving brother to inherit the estate, and if the brother has passed, for the estate to go to his family. When Aunt Josephine died, a few years after my dad's death, my maman flew to South Africa to take care of her affairs. When she rang me a few days later, she was in a terrible state.

At the reading of the will, it was discovered that Aunt Josephine had left everything to her sister and not my brother and me—not, as my mother understood it, because of any particular preference for her sister over my dad and his descendants, but because as heirs to her estate, Jean-Christophe and I were not "blood family." This was the term Aunt Josephine used. My mother was furious and terribly upset.

I was merely baffled. I couldn't understand how someone could think this way. Why base everything, or anything, for that matter, on blood? We had been close! She had liked us! We thought she had loved us. In my angrier moments, I fumed that

I didn't want any of her shit anyway, and who cared about this woman we hardly ever saw or spoke to. But the truth is it still hurt. It was a shocking reminder of how, no matter how secure an adoptee might feel, they can still be regarded within a family as "less than."

With the new law, an adult adoptee wanting to find out about their origins had to apply to the newly created Conseil National pour l'Accès aux Origines Personnelles, or CNAOP, and this involved a fearsome amount of bureaucracy. There would be copious forms to fill out and a trip to France to undertake, and the waiting time would be significant. But still, two years after the law passed, I flew to Paris and entered the offices of the DDASS, La Direction Départementale des Affaires Sanitaires et Sociales. I wasn't nervous that morning, although I must have had adrenaline coursing through my system as I approached the woman at the desk. "Can I help you?" she asked. I told her I lived in the United States and had come back to France to recover my adoption file. "I want to find out about my birth mother," I said.

"Yes," she said wearily. "There is a whole procedure." She started to reel off requirements, all the hoops through which I would have to jump before I could get my hands on the file. It would take weeks, if not longer, and I would have to come back to the office many times. "I can't wait that long," I said. "I have to get back to the U.S." She started to ask me questions, about my life and my past and what I knew of my background. I told her about my parents, my work, the tiny bit of information I had about my birth mother—little more than the fact she might have had blonde hair and blue eyes, which my mother had told me.

The woman at the DDASS and I talked for what seemed like a long time. As the conversation drew to a close, she looked at me and said something unexpected. "I can see there's a kindness in you, and that you're not here with anger." I said that's true, I have no anger toward anyone. She must have taken a liking to me, because what happened next is the sort of thing I never think happens in France. A corner was cut. An official procedure was ignored. Lowering her voice, she said, "Let me see what I can do." Then she asked for my birth name—"Dominique Michele," I said—and told me to call her in a month, she would try to recover my file. And that is precisely what she did.

I have your file in front of me now." I was in my house in LA, the phone clenched to my ear, the California light pearly outside my French window. "You have two older siblings, a boy and a girl. Your birth mother lived in an orphanage until the age of seventeen."

This is how it began; the unfurling of the story untold, read down the line by a kind woman in an office who had no particular reason to help me. Life is strange. Life is strange and one can only be grateful.

My mother had been right: the woman who gave birth to me had blonde hair and blue eyes. She was described as "very Aryan looking." There was a lot of paperwork. It was an unusually large file, owing to my birth mother's long and troubled relationship with the French welfare agencies, which started on the day she was born.

She was not a wanted child. My birth mother was born at the tail end of World War Two in a town in the Ardennes region of France, not far from the border with Belgium. At the time of her birth, the area was occupied by Germans, and immediately after being born, my birth mother was abandoned and admitted to an orphanage. There was no record of who her parents had been, but it seemed likely, the report indicated, that she was what the French call a "Boche baby"—the illegitimate child of a French woman and a German soldier.

I had learned about Boche babies in history class. They were a source of terrible shame to the women who bore them. These children often had difficult early lives, growing up stigmatized while their mothers were shunned by their communities. Most of these babies would grow up never knowing who their German fathers were, and in many cases, never knowing their mothers. Many of them were abandoned at birth. There was no record of how my birth mother fared at the orphanage, but at seventeen, she was discharged. I assume she had nowhere to go.

The next time she turned up in the welfare agency's paperwork, she was living in Versailles and had had two children. Both had been taken away from her. The reasons why were unclear, but a social worker noted she seemed deeply unhappy and took no care of herself. I let this sink in. I had been prepared for a sad story, but this was unimaginable.

One of the pieces of paperwork in my file was a birth certificate—my real one. The only birth certificate I had seen prior to this was the one given to my parents by the orphanage, according to which I had been born in Saint-Germain-en-Laye, a leafy suburb of Paris. There is no explaining this, but I had always had a strong sense it was wrong. I just knew I wasn't born in Saint-Germain-en-Laye; it didn't feel right.

It wasn't until months later, when I had a copy of my birth certificate in my hands, that the information began to fall into place. There was my name, Dominique Michele. There was my birth mother's name. Where the father's name should have been was a blank—all I had ever heard about him was the rumor that he was a businessman from north Africa—and then in the section for place of birth, this: "né à Versailles." What I didn't know until that moment was that in the mid-1960s, when a child in France was adopted it was common for the government to generate a new birth certificate, one bearing the name of the adoptive parents and on which the child was given a new birthplace. This new birth certificate was the one kept officially on file, as a measure to protect the adoptive family from being traced or tracked down by the child's birth parents.

Reading my place of birth, I felt the full rush of having my instincts confirmed. I hadn't been born in Saint-Germain-en-Laye at all. I had been born in Versailles.

Perhaps this sounds trivial, but knowing where you were born is so fundamental to the story of your life that accommodating a change is like finding out your birthday is on a completely different day from the one you had always celebrated. (My birth date, at least, hadn't changed.) For a second, the world spun around me.

I had always insisted to my parents that I had once lived in Paris and they had told me this wasn't the case. As far as they knew, I had been born and abandoned in the suburbs. You were in the orphanage in Versailles, they said; you were born in Saint-Germain-en-Laye and you never lived in Paris. But I always felt that I had been in Paris as a baby. I just knew it.

And there it was in the paperwork: a record of where I lived with my birth mother for the first six months of my life, when she had desperately tried to hang on to me. We had been in an apartment in the center of town, near the Marais, before moving on to the 17th arrondissement.

This is the saddest part of the story. Unlike her own mother, who had abandoned her at birth, my birth mother seems to have fought hard to keep her children. She found a job as a housekeeper cleaning expensive houses in Versailles. She found an apartment for us both, and a babysitter to leave me with when she traveled out to her job every day. Then one day, when I was six months old, she simply didn't come back. No one could reach her, not the babysitter or the social workers. The police were called. I was recovered from the apartment and turned over to the orphanage in Versailles.

No one knows where she went or why she vanished. Once she had abandoned me, the law gave her one year to apply to take me back, after which she would lose parental rights. The year elapsed, and I was adopted by my parents. I assumed she hadn't tried to find me, but then I began to read her letters.

I have never seen a photo of my birth mother. The closest I have come to seeing her is through her handwriting. I have held the paper she touched, the letters she wrote, trying in vain to retrieve her baby.

Her handwriting was quite beautiful. It may not have been hers, of course. She used very proper French, and I have sometimes wondered if someone wrote the letters for her. The replies from the authorities are on file, too. They are emotionless, devoid of sympathy. The authorities, in a cursory fashion, present her with a long list of measures she might take if she wants to start an appeal. It is clear, reading the correspondence, that for my mother to have launched an appeal to recover me would have required an interaction with the French legal system that almost certainly would have been beyond her education and means. It is also apparent, reading the letters, that she was regarded as a disposable human being. The more I learned, the more my heart ached for her, even though I knew that had she succeeded in winning me back, it would have been a disaster for me.

The risk adoptees take if they choose to view their birth records is that it could change the way they look at themselves and at the world. Though I felt tremendous sympathy for the woman who had abandoned me, what I took away from the file was confirmation of what I had always known about myself: That I was tremendously lucky. That I had been born under a good star. I could have been left in the orphanage. I could have been recovered by my birth mother and abandoned, again. My life could have ended up like hers, ransacked, I assumed, by transient men, about whom no records had been kept. I think of my birth mother, seventeen and adrift in the city, and imagine a man coming up to tell her she's beautiful. I imagine her welcoming the love after a loveless childhood. She was totally vulnerable and I don't blame her for any of it. What good does that do?

Occasionally, I'll go back and reread the paperwork. When I first read it, I felt mostly detached. I tried to connect with the story, but it was like I was reading about somebody else. Over the years, my relationship with the information has changed, becoming more nuanced and less colored by shock. The fact that my birth mother did try to get me back from the orphanage has become important. I assume, on the last day she was with me in our apartment, something happened to her—either she got sick, or some other misfortune occurred—that prevented her from coming back for me. She had a job and a home, and seemed to be trying so hard; it hurts me to imagine how losing me must have felt.

A few years after I first read my file, a strange thing happened. I was in Paris, wandering around the city in the sun one day, when I found myself in the 4th arrondissement, in the Marais. I had a sudden, acute emotion, and, looking up, realized that the building in front of me was the address where I had briefly lived with my birth mother. I stood there for a long time, staring up at the window, trying to imagine what had happened within: a woman trying and failing to care for her baby.

She is still alive, I feel it. And I assume I will meet her one day. But as it is now, I have no desire to find her. Tracking her down doesn't feel right. After that first call, during which the kind woman in the office read me my file, I picked up the phone and called my maman in Brittany. I didn't go into much detail about what I had heard. It was a lot for her to take in, and while she had been totally supportive of my desire to recover my file, it was still hard. I was very mindful of her feelings.

I told her a bit about the circumstances of my abandonment and the things I had discovered about my birth mother. And then I told her what it made me feel: that I would always be grateful to have found her and my dad and for the fact that they had welcomed me into their life. While I was telling the story, I didn't call her "my birth mother." I called her "this woman." This woman had been through a lot, I said, but my parents were my parents. They took care of me. Nothing I had discovered changed that, and while there are endless ways to look at the story of my origins, every time I think of it I come back to this: I'm so lucky.

Twelve

THE ACCIDENT

After eight years in LA, I wanted to go back to San Francisco. It was time. I had loved the weather and the beach and I had loved the healthy lifestyle in LA. But there was also a lot to dislike about the city; the surface-deep judgments, the jostling for position, the importance of money and displays of wealth. I was relatively immune to the rat race, but it was wearing after a while. However much I enjoyed aspects of LA, it would never be home the way San Francisco was. At heart I'm a cold-water fish.

Finding the right job, however, was going to be difficult. After quitting Abode, I wanted to leave the city immediately and went to talk to my contacts at the InterContinental Hotel. I knew I wasn't suited long-term to working in a large hotel kitchen, but my experiences at Abode had unsettled me. It was as near as I'd come to opening a restaurant of my own, and it had been a disaster. Until I recovered my nerve, I wanted the security of working for professional managers, not fly-by-night investors who disappeared when things went wrong.

As I have learned, there are pros and cons to working for a hotel chain. Having the infrastructure of a large corporation behind you—handing over the time-consuming business of insurance and payroll and all the things that had caused friction between me and the investors at Abode—frees you up to focus exclusively on cooking. On the other hand, your freedom is cramped by layers of upper management and hotel managers who don't like to take risks.

When the InterContinental Hotel in San Francisco approached me with a job offer, it seemed in some ways a good fit. I would be in charge of creating a new restaurant, a concept in Californian-Italian cuisine, and I could use it as a vehicle for moving back to the city. I would be the boss and could hire Juan Contreras as my chef de cuisine. And I was assured I would be given leeway to make decisions in the kitchen without interference from hotel management.

The restaurant, which was to be called Luce, was being built from scratch. The kitchen of a large hotel has very particular physical requirements because the volume of food being produced is so large. As well as the restaurant itself, we would be fielding room service orders, a constant barrage of demands on the kitchen staff that would require careful thought about space. We would have to think about flow, and the positioning of workstations, to ensure people didn't get under one another's feet. I was excited to sit down and start planning.

A few weeks after leaving Abode, I moved back up the coast, went to inspect the Luce site, and gasped. I was expecting a shell. Instead, the kitchen had already been built, without any consultation with me. The designers had made every mistake it was possible to make. The space was open-plan, but all the cooking stations were crammed against the wall. A single tiny area had been designated for room service, which amounted to some five hundred covers a day. Meanwhile, an entire area had been reserved to cook pasta. It made no sense. There was no flow, no logic. I had mentioned to management that they needed to put in French-style stoves, which have a flat top useful for keeping plates warm when you are serving a tremendous volume of food. Instead, they had fitted traditional stoves with open-flame burners.

And so it went on. While no expense had been spared on the dining room, in the kitchen every corner had been cut—a false economy, by the way, since once we opened, all the equipment would keep breaking and we would constantly be on the phone with maintenance. I had taken the job at Luce because my faith in my own judgment had collapsed and I'd convinced myself I still had a lot to learn before I was ready to go out on my own. It was a pragmatic decision, but it was also a decision made out of fear. During those first days at Luce, I felt some of my old defiance return. If I ever ran my own restaurant, however much

I messed up I surely couldn't do worse than the spectacle un-folding before me.

I moved things around as best I could, but ultimately the space wasn't up to the job and all I could do was try to reduce the pressure on the kitchen by streamlining the menus. I made the room service menu tasty but simple—pizza, hamburgers, sandwiches—similar to the lunch menu and straightforward to prepare. And then I turned my attention to the dinner menu.

During my years at the Manhattan Country Club, I had developed a style of cooking that relied heavily on the promotion of local and sustainable agriculture, and I assumed this would be an even more rewarding approach in San Francisco, where the farm-to-table movement had partly been born. I asked around for recommendations, then began regularly visiting lo-cal farmers and small food suppliers.

One of these suppliers was the Passmore Ranch in Slough-house, near Sacramento, an eighty-six-acre facility run by Michael and Vandy Passmore. Historically, the ranch, which encom-passes a series of open lakes, had specialized in sustainable fish farming and caviar production, but it had recently begun plant-ing vegetables, cultivating miner's lettuce, bronze fennel, ice plants, and radish greens. When the snap peas had a particu-larly lush blossom or the tiny tomatoes were perfectly formed, Michael would call me with a heads-up.

I also met with a farmer named Greg Glosser on his ranch in Pleasant Grove. He sold part of his crop—quince, pome-granate, and other fruits—to Zuni Café in San Francisco, and he began planting ground cherries and Iraqi watermelon for me, and eventually a lot more. It is the strength of these kinds of partnerships that can make or break a good restaurant.

The dishes that came out of these visits were an early expression of a style that would eventually culminate in the menu at Atelier Crenn. I tried to combine flavors in a way that recontextualized familiar ingredients and told a small story on the plate. At Luce, the dish Ocean and Land, for example, was a roulade made of raw beef wrapped around smoked sturgeon, mussels, and arctic char, with black olive ice cream on the side. I served mussels with saffron and spring garlic–flavored broth, and a seafood stew loaded up with peas, zucchini, fish, and lobster. The linguine I served came with a shellfish cream sauce with mandarin-flavored olive oil, trout caviar, and grapefruit.

Outside the restaurant, I tried to reach out to other chefs, to crowdsource our approaches and knowledge. Early on at Luce, I came up with a dinner series I called "A Moveable Feast: 12 Chefs Celebrate 6 Farmers in a Series of Seasonal Suppers." I love these kinds of events, in which chefs come together to celebrate their combined expertise. It ran against the stuffy tradition of high-profile chefs jealously guarding their recipes. At Luce, openness was everything. It can be hard to get traction when you're running a hotel restaurant, but only a year after opening, we were starting to get noticed. *Esquire* magazine named me Chef of the Year in 2008. In spite of my grumbles about the kitchen, everything seemed to be going swimmingly. And then, in 2009, I was invited to appear on *Iron Chef America*.

W hen I got the call from the Food Network, I didn't hesitate to say yes. I had done a small amount of TV before—very short cooking demonstrations on local TV stations, which I had enjoyed. I found the performance aspect fun and felt fairly natural in front of the cameras.

The original Japanese *Iron Chef* was a slightly different beast than the watered-down American version, but the format of the two shows was the same: every week, a guest chef competed against one of the show's regular Iron Chefs in a timed contest presided over by a panel of judges, and complicated by the introduction of a mystery ingredient. In the original Japanese show, these ingredients tended to be more esoteric than in the Western version—swallows' nests and shark fins spring to mind—and the lengths to which the competitors went was more extreme. In one memorable episode, a competitor had cooked and discarded over a thousand dollars' worth of lobster just to provide a hint of flavor to his asparagus.

The American version of the show, then entering its eighth season, was less flamboyant, tending toward kitchen staples for the mystery ingredient, but it still had a theatrical style. Most of the competitors brought with them a fierce performance energy, and I was no different. Watching my episode now makes me laugh. My expression in the early stages is cartoonishly harsh and seems to suggest: "You think you're going to kick my ass? Well guess what? I'm going to kick yours"—which is exactly what I was thinking. In the run-up to filming, Juan and I had stayed up late at the restaurant to work on our prep. We did timed drills, giving ourselves sixty minutes to complete a series of challenges, as per the show, ultimately bringing our time down to forty-five minutes. This, I judged, would allow us to make mistakes and still potentially win.

My opponent that day was Michael Symon—a formidable chef, bestselling author, and owner of Lola Bistro in Cleveland and Sara's in Vegas. His style is very different from my own. It was going to be an interesting battle, particularly when the secret ingredient was revealed to be yogurt.

Symon made bread and meatballs and lamb shank. I made fried yogurt with grilled fig, beets, and rainbow carrots—"an entire garden on a plate," as the host put it. Then I made a series of vegetable-based dishes, including cucumber broth and compressed melon with baby scallop. I dehydrated rose and hibiscus petals to make a hibiscus syrup with yogurt mousse. Everything I made was light, bright, and fresh.

To be a chef is to be a leader, and it requires a robust ego. But there is a difference between good and bad arrogance, and though during the filming of the show I felt full of well-founded confidence, the pressure did get to me once. Unusual for me, I took it out on Juan, snapping at him to hurry up. He was under tremendous pressure too, but instead of snapping back, said quietly, "Don't push me, chef." Those mild words were enough to yank me out of my rudeness and the tension diffused.

The cooking itself went by in a blur. I felt full of adrenaline,

Iron Chef America!

the way I used to feel as a kid when I was taking exams, and when we won the show, I was ecstatic. I had always believed that if you tried your hardest and stayed true to your vision, you would end up being rewarded.

The studio that I had bought when I'd first moved back to San Francisco was in a brand-new condo building and everything in it was pristine. The walls were white, the floor was polished wood, and the bathroom was full of beautiful marble. But I was working eighteen-hour days at Luce, and when I got home I barely had the energy to take a shower before collapsing into bed. One night, I was even more tired than usual, and rather than undressing in the bedroom as I usually did, I threw off my clothes on the bathroom floor. Then I did something that would probably end up saving my life: I dropped my phone on top of my clothes.

The memory of what happened next still terrifies me. Getting out of the shower, I slipped on the wet porcelain and cut my knee so severely it sliced my patellar tendon in half. I was too shocked to feel pain. I passed out. When I opened my eyes, I looked down and was horrified. There was blood everywhere. I couldn't move. Looking frantically around the bathroom, there, by some miracle, was my phone, not quite within reach. I grabbed hold of one end of my sweater and wrapped it around my knee to make a tourniquet. Thus bandaged, I could get up a little to grab for my phone.

I called Juan before calling 911. I needed to hear his voice in that moment of darkness and fear. But he wasn't answering, so after leaving a voice message (that would later plunge him into panic—he said I sounded completely deranged), I came to my senses and called for an ambulance.

I had no idea how badly injured I was. I was in pain and couldn't move, but the shock had yet to wear off and the full situation wasn't clear to me. My two dogs were barking so loudly the dispatcher could hardly hear what I was saying, and when the ambulance arrived, the paramedics couldn't open the door and had to come in through a smashed window. Even then I didn't understand the severity of my situation. I told the paramedics rather matter-of-factly that I had cut myself and saw them exchange glances; it was only later they told me that another thirty minutes of bleeding unattended on the floor and I might have been in very serious trouble.

The next thing I remember is waking up in the hospital. The doctors had given me morphine and told me that the tendon was cut cleanly and they had been able to stitch it together. It was while I was trying to absorb this information that they said something horrifying: to fully recover, I would need three months of bed rest. Three months! And this is when the real nightmare began.

During our first year of business, the management at Luce had been relatively well-behaved. The general manager at the hotel was great and, apart from the kitchen, we hadn't had any real disputes.

It was still a large corporation, however, and when you have an accident like this, management simply doesn't know how to react. Or rather, it knows exactly how to react, and that is as if you're a number. It's black-and-white. There's a total lack of humanity. As far as they were concerned, I was costing them money and they wouldn't be the tiniest bit flexible in helping me.

Since Luce opened, I had been working hundred-hour weeks. Within a year, I would win them a Michelin star—my first. But instead of protecting their investment—as they themselves might have seen it—or being human—as I saw it—they told me coldly that I could have a short, statutory time off at full pay, after which I would be on reduced wages. They told me that "if your paperwork checks out, you'll get workers' comp, but if you're not at work on Monday at seven a.m., don't expect to be paid on Friday." I sat in the hospital bed, staring at the phone in disbelief. I just kept saying, over and over, "What are you talking about?" Say what you like about France, but at least the worker is protected there. And because I was technically a boss, I had no union protection. Appealing to management was my only recourse.

And so I did what people all over this country do when they aren't given sufficient time off to heal. I took the pain meds. I let the doctors patch me up and I got back to work as quickly as humanly possible. I rang my mother in France, and she was shocked, too. "They're not treating you right," she said.

All of this came as a very big blow. I could never have

expected something so cursory and ungenerous. After my accident, I had to rely on the generosity of my friends. A friend who had recently moved from LA to San Francisco put a bed in my living room and helped me out during those months, acting as my crutch when I needed to go to the bathroom and helping me in and out of the shower. I watched a lot of movies and read a lot of books, and by the end of the month, I was going crazy.

Though I would have scar tissue for life where the tendon had been severed and would never completely regain motion in my leg, the biggest consequence of the accident was psychological. For years I had been putting off starting my own restaurant, too anxious and unsure to take the plunge. Now all that changed. Whatever happened, I vowed, I would never be in a situation of dependence like this again.

I realized what I needed to do was to create a space—my space—that was safe for me and my staff. That was the bottom line. I wanted a restaurant in which I could create unhindered, and that meant a place of freedom, of liberty, of humanity. I was done with external management. If I was going to mess up, at least let me mess up on my own terms. I couldn't go on working for people who didn't care about my welfare.

This realization felt huge. I had spent years resenting the people I worked for without things ever having come to a head. Now, the sheer relief of understanding I couldn't go on working this way overwhelmed the more difficult aspects of my recovery.

I felt the moment should be marked. I'd gotten my first tattoo when I arrived in San Francisco, a pair of wings on my upper left arm to represent a free spirit. Since then, I'd had another one done, a flag of Brittany I'd commissioned in homage to my parents. Now, I thought, it was time for a third.

There was a Brazilian tattoo artist whom I admired very much, and three months after my accident, I went in to see him. I wanted something very simple, I said; just my name in Arabic, to symbolize this moment of self-actualization. My name has never been an entirely fixed property, and rendering it in Arabic felt, to me, like recognition of the fact that we have multiplicities within us. Between who I might have been and who I was able to become lay all the freedom of the world. I was ready for the next evolution.

Thirteen

FAMILY MATTERS

In the months after my accident, while still toiling away at Luce and spending every weekend looking for venues that might be suitable for my own restaurant, I met someone who would change the course of my life and the shape of my family. Katherine and I couldn't have been more different; she was a psychologist whose family had been in the U.S. for generations; I was a nomad of uncertain origin. Her medium was words; mine was cooking. She was highly organized and practical; I was neither of those things.

After being introduced by friends in the restaurant industry, however, we immediately hit it off. (Actually that's not quite true. When we first met, I thought she was arrogant. "I think I met you before," I said, after we'd been introduced, and she said, "Oh yeah, everybody tells me that.") But soon enough we were seeing a lot of each other.

Katherine is one of the most intelligent women I've ever met. She's very layered. She's witty. She's kind. She's complicated. She can be stubborn. She's inspiring, yet sometimes drives me crazy. She's the kind of friend you want to have in your corner when things go wrong and you can't see a way out.

I'm convinced that Atelier Crenn would have come into being no matter what my trajectory had been. But in those early days of planning, it was tremendously helpful to have Katherine by my side. She didn't just blandly support my ambitions. She was honest about her doubts, and this forced me to double down on my convictions. "Oh, wow, that sounds great," she said when I sketched out my idea of the restaurant to her. "So, what's your plan B? If it doesn't work, what else will you do?" I was astonished. I had never fully considered this before, what would happen if the restaurant failed. "I don't have a plan B," I said. "It will work."

This is not how a lot of people think, I know. But I can't operate any other way. My philosophy for living is, Why focus on things not working out? There is no failure in life, only opportunity. I believed in myself and I believed in my vision and I was willing to absorb any amount of disappointment to realize it. A few years later, when I did a TEDx Talk in San Francisco, I said, "I don't believe in perfection. I believe in evolution," and this is as close as I can come to explaining how I think. I wasn't being reckless. My plan B was simply to keep pushing, and if things didn't work out, to go back to the beginning and find another way of doing them.

A t the end of 2010, Juan and I were still working at Luce, spending every day off touring venues around the Bay Area while I tried to drum up some investors. At the best of times, opening a restaurant is difficult. It is a high-stakes operation with huge running costs and narrow margins. In San Francisco, the market is crowded and you have to be either exceptionally good, exceptionally novel, or exceptionally lucky to stand out. But only a few years out from the 2008 financial crisis, investment was particularly thin on the ground.

Luce had been awarded a Michelin star in 2009, but in spite of this track record, I was still considered a risky proposition to investors, as a female chef in an industry where most top chefs and most business owners were still men. The concept that Juan and I had for the restaurant was not exactly commercial, either. I knew that I didn't want a starchy, uptight, formal dining room. And I knew that I didn't want a conventional menu.

Finally, after what seemed like years of searching, we found an empty property in Oakland that seemed more or less suitable and we signed a lease. This was it! This was going to be our restaurant, the place I had been dreaming of since I first conceived of becoming a chef. Juan quit Luce, and I semiquit—I would stay on as a consultant, just to pay the bills—giving us time to set about finding investors.

At the last minute, however, we had second thoughts about the venue. It was a new development, a bit too bland and commercial for our purposes, and we backed out of the lease, leaving us scrambling to find somewhere else. An old business acquaintance of mine told me about a space on Fillmore Street, in the Cow Hollow neighborhood of the city. It wasn't an area I particularly liked and the venue itself, while small and cozy, was also worn out. But the building was owned by a Japanese couple who'd had it in their family for a hundred years and this seemed like an encouraging sign. It wasn't a rational assessment, it was an emotional one: I liked the idea of one family owning the place for so long and I felt very connected to the story. We signed the lease and were on our way.

Or at least we almost were. The renovation effort was intense. The venue had been standing empty for a year, before which it had operated as a café for almost two decades. The kitchen was in a terrible state. There was a crust of ancient oil in the fryers. Every piece of equipment was clapped-out. For weeks, Juan came in every day with a mask and threw out all the debris and junk, but there wasn't a lot we could do about the major appliances. We couldn't afford to replace them, not even the lumbering twelve-year-old stove and hood. We would have to make the best of it.

Money was a constant battle. One of our early investors fell through at the last minute and in my panic and desperation, I jumped too quickly to secure a new set of partners. Looking back, I was naive. I was as inexperienced in business as I was confident in the kitchen, and I made a serious mistake. I signed

The kitchen at Atelier Crenn.

a contract that gave my investors reason to believe they had a global right to my name. They demanded a cut of anything I wrote, created, produced, or appeared in, be it a book, set of recipes, or TV show. By the time I realized my error and fought to renegotiate the contract, it was too late. "We own you," said one of the investors.

I turned to Katherine to keep me sane. Throughout the planning period of Atelier Crenn, Katherine had given me every encouragement. When I was frustrated with my business managers or how long the contractors were taking, she talked me down. She encouraged me to stand my ground while staying calm and managing my feelings. The financial risk of opening a restaurant at the tail end of a recession seemed at times unbearable, and although Katherine is more cautious than me, in a crisis she is calm and reassuring. After talking to her, I rationalized away the worst of my fears, persuading myself that just as my confidence could at times be exaggerated, so, too, could my anxieties. Trouble with the investors would rumble on through the opening months and years of Atelier Crenn, but in the meantime I tried to focus on what mattered: the restaurant itself and what I wanted it to achieve. I just had to keep a clear head and focus on opening.

Katherine's greatest gift to me, however, was simply being the woman I loved. As the dining room took shape, she would stop by after work and I would bring a glass of wine and join her at a table. I would write dishes while she watched and tell her she was the inspiration behind them. This wasn't a line. I'm very inspired by love.

As I began to develop the concept for the restaurant, I thought back to those visits with my dad and Albert Coquil to the Michelin-starred restaurants of Brittany and Paris. I thought of my culinary heroes, Olivier Roellinger and Michel Bras. I reflected on how to represent the natural world on the plate and interweave it with my own story.

The word "journey" is overused, but that is how I conceived

of the dishes that Juan and I started to develop for the inaugural menu. In my head, I went back to the fish market in Port de Douarnenez, hearing la criée, the cries of the fishermen, smelling the sharp smell of salt and fresh fish. I revisited my mother's kitchen, where I hungrily awaited the homards bleus, the bright blue lobsters that swarm off the coast of Brittany with which my mother would make lobster bisque. I would substitute the blue lobster of Brittany with the fire-engine red of the native lobsters of San Francisco. In place of the cream from my uncle's cows, I would use bone marrow custard. I would look forward and backward at once.

Perhaps I have been doing this all my life—trying to merge the before with the after so that the different layers of being might come together. I thought of how important the concept of lightness is to me. I believe in harmony—in the idea that the greatest density of experience can feel more like weightlessness. This is what I hoped to achieve with the dishes that I conceived of for our opening run.

While Juan and I deliberated over every detail of the restaurant's menu, décor, seating, and ambience, there was one aspect of our venture that never needed discussion. During my years of dreaming, I had always known that when I opened a restaurant, I would call it Atelier Crenn, not after me but after my father—specifically, after the studio at the back of our summer house in Locronon where he had spent so many hours painting. The word "atelier" in French translates most accurately as "workshop," and this perfectly described my approach. I wasn't creating a finished product. I was creating something that might grow and change as the years went by, a space in which everyone who came into it might develop and find joy. A family, in other words.

Welcome in . . .

Summer has come with its cool breeze.
I touch the salted water, and hold the shell
against my ear.
Like a little widness swimming and leaving
    a beautiful reflection
Oceanic feeling and distilled and pure, love those
    black pearls

There came a wave of an oceanic delicatene
Strolling on the ~~beach~~ beach, in its whimsically
ebullient and red umami

    When the broad Ocean leans softly
against the Spanish land

A first draft of our "menu"…

PART THREE

PART THREE

Fourteen

ATELIER CRENN

I was forty-five when I opened Atelier Crenn—in my prime, for sure, although women aren't assumed to have a professional prime quite like men. Sometimes I get the sense that women over forty aren't even supposed to be visible. Well, with respect, screw that. I was ready. I hadn't waited this long to open my own restaurant to give way on the things I thought really mattered.

I knew what I wanted, and I was willing to fight for it in the face of opposition. The first fight was over tables. We opened with fourteen tables, which I thought was too many and my investors thought was too few. (When, a couple of years later, I finally got rid of the investors, I brought the number of tables down to eight.) A three-hundred-seat restaurant is like a cruise ship; it requires a lot of labor and entails a lot of waste. When you have a smaller restaurant, you're more focused on quality

The interior of Atelier Crenn's dining room.

and keeping the experience intimate. If I could have gotten away with it, I'd have put a counter in the kitchen with only ten seats, but at least with fourteen tables, I knew it would be just about possible to meet every diner and to ensure I had a real encounter with each of them. The human connection was just as important to me as the food itself.

The dining room was designed along clean Japanese lines. The colors were muted but friendly—no stark white tablecloths or harsh lighting. I wanted rugs on the floor and earth tones on the walls, dotted with my father's paintings and presided over by a feeling of zen and tranquillity. The tables were wood, sourced from a sustainable logging company in Portland. The service was discreet and unpretentious. I've been in fine-dining restaurants where the atmosphere is so strained you're scared to breathe or pick up a glass, lest you drop it. Excessive attention from servers can make it hard to relax. That's not what we were trying to do. We were trying to make it informal and fun.

Atelier Crenn opened on January 21, 2011. The night before, everyone I loved came to celebrate. My nerves had returned with a vengeance, and in the days before the official opening I had convinced myself hordes of people were hoping I'd fail. I'm not vulnerable to impostor syndrome, but every night that week I lay awake imagining their response: who does this person— this woman who never went to cooking school or set foot in a commercial kitchen before the age of twenty-five—think she is?

If the adrenaline of the following night hadn't displaced the terror, the sheer amount of love coming my way would have. Everyone I knew from every part of my life seemed to be in the room that evening. Katherine was there, of course, and many of my chef friends from other restaurants, and Melinda, with a gang of people I had known since my earliest days in the city. I made a speech in which I thanked everyone for their wonderful show of friendship. I said it was a strange experience, unveiling something I'd been working on for so many years. I can't remember what else I said; seeing a restaurant bearing my father's name was simply overwhelming. I had been a chef for over two decades and suddenly I felt like an ingenue.

Winter has come with its cool breeze
See: the efflorescing beauty with rosy cheeks rises
With a most adored gift from Neptune, this aureate bloom
Warriors ashore bathe in a glow as luminous as its gilded crown
To bury in fallen leaves my treasures of the earth and sea
By the shimmer of black pearls, tumbling in the ashen cloud
An armored gent listens, beneath the bluff
As delicate creatures of green and blue surface to bloom
For a melody faintly heard in a golden haze, the light of fog
And the verdant bounty of the gatherer's harvest in caring hands

Soon comes an arboreous scent, as I walk amongst the giants
Gleaming through the canopy, an orb so felicitous and splendid
Winter has come and is full of sweet surprises
Sweetness, bounty, thanks

Our "menu"… the poem we present to our guests.

s a concept, the tasting menu relieves diners of the need to
make choices, allowing them to give themselves up to the
flow of the evening. It introduces them to food they might not
have ordered themselves and injects an element of surprise into
the meal. In the case of Atelier Crenn, this was aided by the
indirectness of the printed menu, which only hinted at what
diners would see on the plate. I had given the restaurant the
subtitle Poetic Culinaria, meaning that the experience of dining
there could be regarded as somewhat akin to reading poetry, as
a series of expressions by which one might way feel one's way
toward meaning.

I have always enjoyed reading poetry. I love Baudelaire. I
love the American poet Mary Oliver, who wrote so movingly
about nature and the sensual overload of living life to the fullest.
Clearly I'm not a poet like Oliver, but I like putting feeling into
words and pinning the moment to the page. I wondered why
one couldn't be creative in this way when writing a menu, and
as Juan and I started to develop the look and feel of the restaurant, I started to formulate an idea of a poem instead of a conventional list of dishes. A poem is an expression with words that
takes you through waves of emotion, and that's exactly what my
food is about.

It's not that each line of the menu directly corresponds to a
dish. It is more impressionistic than that. I want to evoke a feeling, to put the diner in a frame of mind that might permit them

to travel with me over the evening's dozen or so courses, through a series of moods and sensations. The menu changes with the seasons and with it the poem, but the first line is always the same—"Summer has come and is full of sweet surprises"—a reference to the Kir Breton I serve at the start of every meal, just as my mother served Kir Breton to her guests at her dinner parties. I might offer oyster next—"under midnight glow, I can taste the sweetness of the sea"—or a floral salad, "the forest radiant with possibility," twisting back around to the ocean and a sea urchin or squid, whereupon "feeling the black sand under my toes, I dreamed of / these creatures' languid movements."

This sort of thing makes people nervous, I know. If people said I was pretentious, which they did, I shrugged it off, listening respectfully without feeling any obligation to change. My sense was that my restaurant wasn't there to hurt anyone and there was an easy fix for those who disliked it. One food critic wrote disdainfully of how much it cost to eat at Atelier Crenn, to which I would say, "So don't come." Another wrote, "Oh, what are Crenn and Contreras going to come up with next, a recreation of the Golden Gate Bridge?" (A reference, I guess, to the elaborate architecture of the food, although honestly, who knows.) Others said snidely that the food was "too beautiful," something I have been hearing all of my professional life. Tant pis.

You can't have fear. You can't think things are too risky. You've got to do what you believe is right for you, otherwise you will never go anywhere. I would never have left France if I had let fear govern my life. And so while I know it's risky to jump off a bridge, being who you want to be is not risky. It's not even a choice. It is the only possible way to live and move forward.

To me Atelier Crenn wasn't outrageous or elitist or pretentious or absurd, it was simple: the idea that, with the right combination of flavors and words, my diners might join me for a walk in the forest. We might stroll through a farm or take a trip to the beach, as their memories moved in the same direction as mine. There we might stand for a moment, side by side at the shore, our ears pressed against the same imaginary shell.

The easiest way to explain how I set about creating the dishes for the first menu at Atelier Crenn is to use the example of the Kir Breton. The classic Kir Breton is an aperitif, a combination of cassis and sparkling cider. I wanted to take that idea, loaded as it was with my memories of home, and turn it into something more unusual, an amuse-bouche in which each of the disparate elements was given its own platform, shining in isolation before coming together.

In the case of the Kir Breton, I wanted guests to start their meal with a pop in the mouth, a small explosion of surprise that set them up for the journey to follow. I toyed with various ideas before settling on a spherical cocoa-butter shell, off-white and perfectly round, with the cider trapped inside and a swirl of cassis on the top. It is light, surprising, a little theatrical, and we always make sure to have a few nonalcoholic versions on hand for those who don't drink. Oh, and with the combination of the ecclesiastical purple and the buttery white globe, it is beautiful, too.

This approach has been called modernist. I don't think of it that way particularly, although I understand why that word might be used. I do like to take things apart before putting them back together, as a way of ringing the maximum flavor out of each individual ingredient. Visually, it also ensures that the greatest variety of color, shape, and texture makes it into a dish, a celebration rather than an elimination of difference.

Imagine a traditional bowl of onion soup, thick, gloopy, and saturated with cheese. I have always found this classic French dish too heavy, although I do like the flavors. For Atelier Crenn, I wanted to do something that was based on onion soup but cleaner and brighter—less of a bog and more of a tide pool. And so I inverted the recipe, putting a thin layer of cheese at the bottom of the bowl, a clear onion broth on the top, onion marmalade around the side, and a skein of sherry vinegar on the surface. It is a dish that is full of bright flavor, a sharpened-up version of a comfy old classic and it is one of my proudest creations.

Let's deal with this business about beauty. In my twenties, I applied for a sous-chef position at the Park Hyatt in San Francisco, and a few days later duly turned up for the interview. All the candidates were taken into the kitchen and asked to make a single dish by way of audition. I did my own thing—I can't even remember what it was now, but I do remember what they said when they rejected me: your plate is too pretty.

The implication is that a chef who spends time on making a plate beautiful is somehow skimping on everything else. It is thought to be frivolous, self-indulgent, irrelevant to the task at hand, as if cooking has nothing to do with aesthetics. It is true that, technically, you don't eat with your eyes. But a good meal can appeal to more than one of your senses. No one would argue that texture doesn't play a crucial role in a meal; no matter how tasty, none of us would be satisfied to eat at a restaurant where everything had the consistency of paste. Nor would we be happy if everything smelled the same way. How a plate looks is, to me, just as important. We're not serving astronaut pellets. All the senses should be fully engaged.

Put it this way: when you dress, you try to put things together in a way that communicates something of your character. It doesn't have to be luxurious, but it does have to be thoughtful. To call a plate beautiful is just another way of saying that there is an emotion contained therein, that it speaks to you when you look at it. For me, a successful meal should have the visual artistry of a painting. It is not enough to simply slap food on a plate. There is no celebration in that. You killed the fish, so you want to bring back its beauty. It shows a certain respect for the sacrifice.

Color is important. I have a dish based around carrot and aloe, which has been designed to look like succulents in the Californian landscape, with a red quinoa "soil," aloe vera gel, and a bright carrot sorbet. These are not outlandish ingredients but rather familiar flavors remade afresh, opening our eyes to the things we see—or rather don't see—every day.

Take the carrot. There is so much story with a carrot. This story can be good or bad. "Baby carrots," for example, those depressing bags you see piled high in the supermarket, are not baby carrots at all. They are regular carrots that have been washed, peeled, and whittled down to a slimy, neon-orange stub, their production entailing a tremendous amount of waste. To eat a carrot—a real carrot—is to feel the soil in your mouth. There's a beauty in that which all good chefs understand. Alain Passard, whose restaurant L'Arpège, in Paris, I visited in 2013, makes a garlic and carrot velouté I still close my eyes to re-member.

One of the early dishes I worked on at Atelier Crenn was simply called Le Jardin. It involved baby carrots—real babies, fresh and young with the soil still clinging—edible flowers, and pea shoots. It looked like a riotous tumble of color and form, a messy artifice that combined cooked, raw, and pickled produce, depending on the season. I used fava beans in the spring, to-mato and avocado in the summer. I made a meringue base that acted almost as an edible plant pot. If I'm honest, it looked more like a garden than a salad, an entire tiny ecosystem on a plate, with basil soil at the root and a bouquet of microherbs at the top, while the lettuces and flowers peeked out of the hollow of each meringue.

In my cooking I have always been drawn to a combination of

the very simple and the very complicated. I cook with Versawhip, a soy-based protein used to stabilize whipped foams. I use kuzu starch, a Japanese starch with a glutinous texture useful for making gnocchi or dumplings. I use nitrogen, the extreme cold of which is useful for sealing in flavor; dehydration has a similar effect. And I use calcium lactate (white crystalline salt used as thickener) and sodium hexametaphosphate (a preservative that helps the hydration process). These aren't just effects. They can be slammed as gimmicks, but there is always a good flavor-based reason for what I am doing.

Sometimes a dish has a superficial simplicity that masks an awful lot of technique underneath. If we go back to that basic unit, the tomato, I might present a dish that strives to get at the essence of the tomato by coming at it from many different angles. I might use a poached tomato, with tomato consommé and tomato compote, and a little shiso sorbet and yuzu panna cotta on the side. (Shiso is a leaf in the mint family; yuzu is a citrus fruit used in Japanese and Korean cooking.) There is a lot going on in this dish, which involves the preparation of five separate elements. Yet on the plate, I try to present it as a play on a simple tomato. This is something visual artists understand better than chefs, perhaps; that a dish of this kind is simultaneously a tomato and an idea of a tomato. The interplay of the two is what I am striving for. It is possible to taste and think at the same time.

A lot of these techniques are incredibly time-consuming and we cook from scratch every day. I like to keep my kitchen quiet.

I don't even like the sound of loud grilling or sautéing, which is one of the reasons why I love the Japanese grill. Some people work with high fire, but the beauty of this particular grill—as with smoking—is that it uses logs to cook the food in slow motion, just kissing the ingredients rather than slamming them around in a pan. Having a quiet kitchen gets you into a different headspace. We sometimes have music on, usually when we do a deep clean after Saturday night service. But my preference is for silence, which respects and understands others as they focus on their work.

The flow of the kitchen schedule took a while to establish but eventually we settled on a way of doing things. Three cooks generally arrive at the restaurant at 9:00 a.m. and start prepping all the things that take longest—stock, soup, sauce, and bread. Most of the ingredients are delivered fresh daily and these deliveries are large and complicated. My dishes tend to have a lot of components, so that for three or four dishes, on average fifteen to twenty separate recipes might be required before everything is pulled together on the plate.

People are curious about the creation of new dishes; where you start and how you know when you're finished. It is a hard thing to talk about in concrete terms. Creating a new dish is, I would guess, equivalent to how an artist creates a painting. You use intuition and guesswork. You feel your way along in the dark. If a new flavor combination speaks to me, it's an almost auditory sensation, one that I find I can hear when it's finished.

Rather like rhythm, I don't think you can learn it. I dream of moving people, as anyone who creates something does.

A good example of this is my signature dish, A Walk in the Forest. It was a dish inspired by the walks I used to take with my father through the forests of Brittany. Every element of the dish corresponded to a sensory memory. There was a scattering of lightly burnt pine meringue, with the freshness and crunch of forest leaves; there was edible soil made from basil and pumpernickel, with the slightest hint of life's bitterness; there was a variety of wild mushrooms—sautéed, pureed, pickled, and dehydrated, reminiscent of the dark funk of the woods—and mushroom broth to represent the light; as well as hazelnut praline and foraged herbs. I can't say in exactly what order the composition came about, and there were a few blind alleys. But you learn as a chef that when something doesn't work, it is merely a stepping-stone toward some other end, often one you can't yet see. When the dish was done, it sang on the plate. My father taught me on those walks about the taste and flavor of life. "Papa, what's that smell?" I would ask, a fistful of fresh earth in my hand. "Mon petit Crenn," he'd say, "that is the scent of a life, long walked but well lived." I think of eating this dish as akin to following a trail, a way into one's own memories of being outside, or an invitation to step into the magical forest of a fairy tale.

Of course, to create something "natural" like this requires an enormous amount of artifice. This particular recipe is a gargantuan undertaking of different moving parts, the basis of which is the rich mushroom broth, which must be prepared before anything else and will be used as a component in the mushroom puree and pickled mushroom. Pumpernickel soil is simply pumpernickel bread put in a dehydrator for three hours until crisp, before being pulsed and seasoned. Mushroom whims are finely sliced king trumpet mushrooms, dried and then baked, and accompanied by mushroom paper (a thin layer of mushroom puree spread across an acetate sheet and dried in a closed oven until crisp). Then there is the pine meringue and the hazelnut praline. Considering the amount of prep that goes into this dish, it may become clear why I had no desire to open a three-hundred-seat restaurant.

At 11:00 a.m., after morning prep, everything is cleaned and scrubbed down, ready for the next phase—the arrival, at noon, of six more cooks. From here, things start to heat up. A meal for the staff is prepared that I insist must be healthy and delicious—not just leftovers—and that different chefs assume responsibility for every day. There is more cleaning at 2:00 p.m., and we all eat together around 3:30, when the front of house staff arrive. Then from 5:00 to 5:30 everything comes together as we prepare to open the restaurant.

I float around the kitchen helping out where necessary. I inspect plates to make sure they leave the kitchen looking as good as they can. Every single plate is checked before it goes out; this is another benefit of not serving six hundred covers a night. Once the diners have settled in and put in their wine orders, my favorite part of the evening arrives. There were those in my circle who, before the restaurant opened, knew I wondered how I would handle being a host. I love to meet people, but I can be blunt and I don't enjoy small talk. I like to connect with people deeply right from the start, and I know that even among those who love me, there were some who thought I'd fail miserably— that I would go in too hard when I spoke to my diners and they wouldn't understand my intention. That I would be like a person talking Arabic to a person speaking Chinese.

This isn't how things turned out. Right from the beginning, people understood intuitively what I was trying to do. When food comes from within, there's a richness of thought and struggle and narrative that makes you vulnerable to others and invites them to be vulnerable with you. It sounds crazy, but one night a woman started crying while eating a turnip. It reminded her of something and she was just overwhelmed. Every human story is connected if you tell it right, and when I cook, there is a connection to some inner part of myself that when things work out is able to touch people.

I started to think more about France. If there is a central irony to my food it is related to the fact that if I hadn't left France I never would have discovered who I was, but discovering who I was took me right back to France. Memory has always been a creative trigger for me, and night after night, as I revisited my roots in the kitchen, I felt a new passion for the place, a strength of feeling inspired, in part, by the deep longing of separation. I hadn't lived in France for over twenty years and it had never seemed closer.

Still, times were tough.

Even with our small number of tables we weren't always fully booked. Business wasn't consistent, making it hard to model a business plan. There was no money for expensive publicists so we had to rely on word of mouth. We wanted fresh flowers every night but flowers are expensive, too, so we decided to do them ourselves. One evening in the first year, I looked at the books and saw we had only five reservations. It would have been too expensive to open for only ten people, so we had to try to get everyone to reschedule. On another slow night, we called diners and made up a maintenance issue (gas leak!) to cancel the seating.

Staffing was difficult. It is hard to hire the best people in the city when you have no reputation to go on. For the first two years, it was a constant rotation of hiring, firing, and rethinking the team, getting rid of one egotistical chef who came to us from abroad and prefaced everything he said with, "Well, when I was in Europe," while fighting to hang on to real stars who got poached. During those first few years, my job was half chef, half human resources manager.

Meanwhile, the issue with my business partners raged on. As the implications of the contract I'd signed became clear, I hired lawyers to try to undo it. The investors tried to marginalize me by saying, "You're an artist, not a businesswoman; we'll take care of the business decisions for you." When it became clear I wouldn't keep quiet, hostility between us escalated. Frequent bullying messages came in via text and email. Meetings between us got more and more awkward.

I would emerge from these encounters in a state of rage. I rarely lose my temper, but I was being pushed to the absolute limit, and once again Katherine would talk me down. She reminded me to be calm and businesslike, and not to take things too personally. She knew me well enough to know I was in danger of focusing on the fight with the investors at the expense of things that mattered more.

It would take five long years of working fourteen-hour days at the restaurant for me to raise the money to buy these people out, the lesson of which is always to read the contract, don't rely on the goodwill of others, and find better lawyers than I had in the first instance. And only go into partnership with people you trust. Creative talent isn't enough. The hard, practical work of setting up a business can't be ignored. I wish it had been different, but there you go. The only way we learn is by making mistakes.

It was all very stressful and I still felt a long way from making a breakthrough. When, a year after opening, the Netflix show *Chef's Table* reached out and asked if they could base an episode around me and come and shoot in the restaurant, I said no; I simply wasn't ready. Two years later, they repeated the offer and it precipitated a rare moment of disagreement between Juan and me.

Juan, who when Atelier Crenn opened had switched from savory to pastry chef, was killing it on the dessert front, and while we may not have been booked to capacity every night, the tide had started to turn. In 2013, two years after opening,

Juan and I in Paris, 2012.

Michelin awarded us two stars. Juan thought we still weren't ready for the cameras—we were fighting with our investors and the restaurant wasn't in good enough shape for that kind of exposure. I disagreed. Sometimes when things aren't going right you have to make a bold gesture, and it seemed like madness to me to send the TV cameras away a second time.

I said to Juan let's go for it, and, overriding his objections, welcomed the cameras in. It was scary for me, not just as a chef-owner promoting my business, but as someone being asked to open up about my life in a way I hadn't done in public before.

The show aired and the impact was immediate and phenomenal. We were 90 percent booked for an entire year. It was our most financially successful year to date and put us on the map internationally, even more so than the Michelin stars. People who watch cooking shows on Netflix don't necessarily dine out all the time or follow the specialist culinary press, so the show brought us a whole new customer base. It also brought us a lot of goodwill, mainly I think because I had been open and vulnerable about where I had come from. I spoke about my adoption and my family, and my mother even appeared in a scene with me. Years after the show aired, people still come into the restaurant and say, "We saw you on *Chef's Table*."

One thing Juan and I had promised each other when we opened Atelier Crenn was that we would always try to see our vulnerabilities as strengths. Being small was a virtue, it made us light on our feet. The same went for all the other decisions we'd made that exposed us to criticism and that wound up being our greatest selling points.

People came around to the poem menu. The avant-garde style of my plates eventually won a great deal of praise. There was one decision I made, however, that still annoys people and from which I refuse to back down. I hate signs. Who invented signs? Why do we need to tell everyone we're here? If people

The exterior of Atelier Crenn, Fillmore Street, San Francisco.

want to find us, they'll find us. At Atelier Crenn, there's no sign on the building announcing the restaurant's name and no sign on the door, either. People get frustrated, walking straight past us or coming in fuming to tell me they drove around the block for ten minutes before finding us. I have a tendency to shrug, I'm afraid. Not having a sign on the restaurant is a little eccentric, I know. But it does something no other measure I can think of will do: it forces people to pay attention from the very beginning.

Fifteen

THE ETHICAL KITCHEN

An hour north of San Francisco in bucolic Sonoma there is a place called Bleu Belle Farm. It is a beautiful spot, dotted with giant old trees, greenhouses, and a chicken coup full of huge, happy hens. Seventy percent of Atelier Crenn's fresh produce is grown there, using biodynamic and organic farming in soil that is regularly tested to ensure there are no chemicals. We as humans have destroyed nature in a way that's so drastic, I feel that even in the smallest, most individual ways, we have a duty to try to restore it.

For me, as a chef, this means creating a menu with the spotlight on vegetables. There is a prejudice among diners that, particularly in a fine-dining restaurant, vegetable dishes don't represent value for money. Part of the ethos of Atelier Crenn is to treat vegetables as reverentially as other restaurants treat meat. Along with fish, they are the heart and soul of what we

Welcome to Bleu Belle Farm.

Life in Sonoma.

do, partly because my taste skews in that direction and partly because, if you are a chef and care about the planet, it seems to me the only possible approach you can take.

As a child, I was never under any illusion as to where the steak or sausages on my plate came from.

From the youngest age, we would stay at my uncle Jean's livestock farm in Brittany, sometimes waking in the morning to the sound of screaming pigs. It was truly terrifying, as was the sight, when I got out of bed to look out the window one time, of my uncle and his workers chasing an already bloodied pig around the yard. As I got older, I understood that, in fact, Uncle Jean's pigs represented the best-case scenario—kindly treated, living in roomy and well-aerated barns, with plenty of good food and as humane a death as could be managed. Every last shred of the carcass was used on my uncle's farm, to make everything from blood sausage and rillettes to head cheese and saucisson. If we have to eat meat, this is the only decent way to do it.

I am not quite a vegetarian, and I don't run a vegetarian restaurant. I do, however, recognize that particularly in America, too many people eat a meat-centered diet, when for health and environmental reasons meat should be a secondary ingredient, one component among many rather than a huge slab at the center of the plate. You don't have to eat a hamburger every day, you know?

It's a simple message: that people should think before they eat and consider where the food on their plate has come from.

The problems of industrial farming are well-known by now—animals crated for their entire short lives, raised in appalling conditions, and stuffed with antibiotics, which after slaughter get into the food chain. I won't buy from these places. We serve pork belly at the restaurant and I source the pork only from farms where the animals are well treated. Likewise our lamb, which comes from a farm up in Marin where the animals are respectfully treated.

The cured meat that goes into our beef carpaccio is Japanese Wagyu, which comes from cattle treated as close to the way my uncle Jean treated his cows as I have managed to find. Wagyu cattle aren't pumped full of hormones or made to spend their entire miserable lives in a pen, and as a consequence, their flavor is better.

I don't serve chicken in my restaurant. This shocks people sometimes. How can any restaurant that doesn't market itself as vegetarian strike one of the major proteins off the menu? The fact is I don't like chicken because I can't find a supplier that meets my standards. The term "free-range" no longer means anything—it is used as a woolly alibi to hide all sorts of cruelty—and it is almost impossible to find a humane and sustainable supplier of poultry you can trust. Instead of chicken, I serve rarer birds such as squab, the more acceptable term for a pigeon in culinary culture, and a delicious halfway house between poultry and red meat. These birds are less likely to be raised in factory-farm conditions and can form the basis of a lovely winter dish I serve with maple syrup, squid ink chips, and parsnip logs.

Pintade is a type of guinea fowl. It is native to Africa, and in the restaurant we serve it with lemon, the citrus giving it a light, slightly Asian flavor. I've always thought of this particular dish as a bridge between different worlds, a meeting of earth tones with the sky. The word "fusion" has become frowned upon as gimmicky and fashionable, but the fact is that most good things involve a fusion of sorts. We take what we know and combine it with unfamiliar things to create something unexpected and new. To me, pintade is a wonderful comfort food—particularly when battered and fried it provides an alternative to traditional fried chicken—and one that we often serve at staff meals. And as my uncle Jean taught me, I try to minimize waste by using every scrap of the bird, stripping it down to the bone, before using the bone itself to make consommé.

Running an ethical kitchen is about more than where you choose to source your meat. It involves making sure that everyone in the restaurant, from front of house to the kitchen, has some sense of connection with nature. It means ensuring that "organic" isn't just a label but connects in everyone's mind to the experience of being on a farm, smelling the soil, understanding that we are part of the chain, not above it. It is about recognizing that when you put something foreign in the earth, you infect the food that is grown there.

Bleu Belle Farm is an emotional place for me, as a chef and as a human being. It's also an important part of the restaurant. Psychologically, I think it's good for the team to be able to walk around the farm once every few weeks, to learn about the soil

A feast at Bleu Belle Farm.

and the trees and to hear the sound of the wind. The pleasures of cooking are as tactile as they are emotional and intellectual, something I have known since my childhood, when raking through the black earth to recover potatoes on my grandmother's farm gave me a physical thrill. I try to re-create this for my staff and to make sure that everyone has a chance to get out to the farm regularly and reconnect with ingredients at a mineral level.

A lot of what we grow there is deeply unfashionable. I love reclaiming unfashionable food. It acts as a surprise on the menu and is an antidote to waste, which is one of the biggest problems in Western food culture. We like to buy cheaply and discard in this country. We eat cheap empty calories that do us no good. Obesity doesn't come from the amount of food that you eat, but rather from the quality of your diet. If you're eating chemicals that are not supposed to be in your body, your body is going to react. If you eat a lot of proper food, you might get big, but you won't get obese.

Food connects to mood, too. When you start to feed people better, they feel better. This has been proven in studies of school-age children. The child who is eating properly will perform better than the child who is not. Well-fed prisoners behave better than prisoners fed on slop and scraps. But there are so many powerful interests invested in discouraging Americans from eating more healthily. When Michelle Obama tried to promote organic farming, the backlash she faced was amazing. And why? Because industrial farming fought back.

Before you buy something, you have to ask yourself if you know what the company stands for, and whether you want to support it. And while I am not a puritan about calories—I love butter, I eat a chocolate croissant for breakfast almost every day, and I love sugar, even though it's killing the world—I do want people to think before they eat, to consider the quality of what they put in their mouths and to expand the range of what are considered "desirable" ingredients.

Take rutabaga, for example. Along with other root vegetables, it is associated with food shortages, particularly in France where it was a reliable staple during the Second World War. I love to take this supremely unfashionable and humble vegetable and pair it with a delicacy like crab, with perhaps an artichoke puree on the side. I love turnip, which we grow copiously at the farm. I will make something like turnip soufflé or turnip crème caramel—yes, it's delicious—in a heartbeat.

Navet is a spicy root vegetable I grew up with, a little like radish and a delicious, much-overlooked ingredient, as is salsify, another dowdy root vegetable that happened to be my father's favorite. It forms the basis of a savory dish I make with white chocolate and cauliflower.

To enjoy all of these ingredients requires one to check one's prejudices and let imagination reign. "Carrot jerky" might sound absurd but it's wonderful. (You soak the carrot in pickling lime to create a skin, cure it to draw out the moisture, brine it to rehydrate, then cook and dehydrate it again.) One might think of the carrot as an ingredient not suited to this kind of

Fresh herbs for the restaurants.

effort—only meat is supposed to be worthy of a many-stage process—but that simply isn't the case. As our meat-heavy diets make us sick and deplete the planet's resources, we have to expand the range of what we understand to be possible, and, as chefs, expand the range of our experience.

Take pickling lime. It is actually water with calcium hydroxide, and I discovered it in Spain, via Chef Andoni Luis Aduriz, and after returning to San Francisco worked on the technique with my former sous-chef, Daniel Beal, until we got it just right. It works for other vegetables as well as carrots and is an agent that has been used for thousands of years to make corn into masa.

Or take a more common ingredient such as honey. When Juan was working on a honey dessert, he got deep into local bee-keeping culture, learning about the engineering that goes into a honeycomb, right down to the difference between "free-form comb building" and guiding bees with plastic comb frames.

He learned how hives from different neighborhoods produce subtly different–tasting honey, in accordance with the plants they feed on. (In Potrero Hill, for example, the honey has a hint of the fennel that grows on the hillside there.) To really finesse his recipe he had to educate himself to the level of expert so that his final dish encompassed honey meringue and beeswax sorbet, and included one and a half ounces of bee pollen. The result was a balance of flavors and textures so finely wrought that it seemed to be an expression of nature without intermediary.

This is the illusion of our kind of cooking; the immense, labor-intensive efforts that go into mimicking the world's natural processes. Consider a dessert Juan makes called The Sea. During the research period for this dish, he went to Monterey to learn about seaweed and algae and came back with a radical dessert, featuring a palate cleanser of pineapple water with algae, followed by a dish of compressed aloe flavored with sea lettuce and shiso. This was served in either mussel, clam, or oyster shells, so that the whole thing looked like a beautiful tide pool.

For a pear sorbet and sage cake with yogurt snow, Juan visited Peter Jacobsen's stunning farm in Yountville, where he found just what he was looking for—Seckel pears—the smallest and sweetest pear in the world that is sometimes referred to as the "sugar pear." This is the beauty of Juan's dessert work: it relies on natural rather than artificial sugars and never goes heavy on the cream.

The fact is that we all have some work to do when it comes to reeducating our palates. That includes me. Foie gras is an emotional part of many French people's diets. For my part, I associate it with precious childhood memories of visiting my aunt Madeleine's house in Lot-et-Garonne, in the southwest of France. She owned a foie gras farm and her birds were free-range; I used to run around the yard with them. I didn't know about gavage back then, the technique of force-feeding birds to fatten the liver for foie gras, but looking back, for all the apparent happiness on my aunt's farm, I know her birds wouldn't have escaped that hideous fate.

And yet I still have an emotional response to good French foie gras. My family would eat it at Christmas, as a side to the turkey along with roast chestnuts, smoked salmon, and oysters, and it featured in an early dish at Atelier Crenn. There are ethical foie gras farms these days, most famously that of Eduardo Sousa in Spain, who has experimented with creating foie gras without resorting to gavage. And I find the outcry around foie gras somewhat absurd, when factory farming creates many more unhappy animals without generating anything like the same protest. But I have evolved, too, and understand that in spite of my happy memories of my aunt Madeleine's farm, I can't condone the cruelty. There is no foie gras on the Atelier Crenn menu these days.

There is also no fish that hasn't been sourced from sustainable outlets. The fishing industry has changed radically since my childhood. La criée no longer exists. Now all fish sales are mediated by distributors. Nostalgia can be deadly, but this seems like a sad passing and it means you have to do your research into where the distributor buys its fish.

Fish stocks are in crisis, too, of course. According to the UN, the annual catch of fish removed from the ocean every year is 40 percent larger than it was 50 years ago. Resources are dwindling. By some estimates, up to 90 percent of the large predatory fish such as cod, shark, and swordfish have been removed from the oceans, which are also under threat from pollution and climate change.

I don't serve large fish like tuna; I prefer smaller fish and shellfish. I try to find sustainable options such as oysters, which are not only delicious but ecologically sound. Oyster farms actually play a restorative role in ocean ecology, creating reefs that serve as a home to lots of other marine plants and animals. Like honeybees and grapes grown for wine, oysters express the character of their surroundings through their individual flavors. I have always loved Belon oysters, thousands of tons of which are transplanted to absorb nutrients from the Belon River in the south of Brittany every year, but I love the California oysters, too—the Kumamoto and Kusshi varieties, both small and exquisite and native to the Pacific Northwest. You are tasting the planet itself when you eat these finely bred shellfish, drawing down into something infinite that goes back to the first sea and beyond.

There is another, more practical, ethical dimension to running a restaurant, and that is the way in which you treat your staff. San Francisco is the most expensive city in the United States, and at Atelier Crenn we have always paid entry-level jobs at above the minimum wage. We pay every intern. If you come here, you work, and I don't want anyone to work for me for free.

We give people 401(k) plans for retirement, and everyone has an annual five days of vacation plus twelve days of personal time. And we allocate paid time off for staff to give their services to charity. That starts at the top—I am working with a charity called the Root Project that aims to replant coffee, cocoa plants, and one million trees in Haiti after the devastation following Hurricane Matthew in 2016. For me, these measures are about reinvesting the profits from the restaurant in the people who have made it successful. We try to do as much as we can.

There is a broader way in which I try to manage an ethical kitchen, and that is by stripping out the underlying presumptions that have kept so many promising women and people of color from realizing their potential as chefs. A critic once wrote of me that I'm successful because I am "attractive and charismatic and cook like a man," a shockingly sexist statement that an editor shouldn't have allowed through. Every day I push back against these judgments at Atelier Crenn the best way I know how: leading by example.

Kitchens can be terribly stressful environments, and I also try to exercise good pastoral care. I insist that everyone on the team sits down and eats a delicious and nourishing staff meal every day. We might have Korean soup with braised beef, or a lamb barbacoa with tacos, followed by freshly baked chocolate chip cookies, and though people eat as fast as they can, everybody does sit down. We made it a requirement to stop work for at least a few minutes. These are family meals that bolster the sense of community that keeps us together during more stressful parts of the day.

Although I finish at the restaurant at 10:00 p.m., I often don't leave until midnight. My kitchen staff is very young, so I try to be there for them as much as possible and to make the atmosphere focused but light. Kindness isn't weakness; you can be strong and professional without being a jerk. We've had people come trail from harsher kitchens—the kind that suck the personality right out of you—and say, "Wow, everyone here is having such fun."

There are good reasons for putting these measures in place. Burnout in the culinary world is a very common phenomenon and depression and alcohol abuse are rife. There are plenty of news stories about chefs cracking under the pressure, most famously Bernard Loiseau, the famous chef at La Côte d'Or in eastern France, who shot himself in 2003 amid rumors that he was about to lose one of his three Michelin stars. Sébastien Bras, the son of my hero Michel Bras and a highly regarded chef in his own right, later opted out of the Michelin system, criticizing it for creating far too much pressure.

When I got my first star at Luce, did I feel pressure? Maybe. I don't know. I think I look at pressure differently than most people. For some successful chefs, the public recognition of being awarded a Michelin star is what they have lived their whole lives for, but for me it was never the endgame. It's a great honor, but I didn't get into cooking for that. I always knew I could live without it.

I remember a discussion I had with Anthony Bourdain in the Cayman Islands a few years ago, in which he talked about his depression and how overwhelmed he felt at times. I didn't know Tony well, but I knew him enough to know he was someone who had carried this struggle for a long time. If you read *Kitchen Confidential*, it is apparent there was something within him he couldn't get past.

I learned that weekend in the Cayman Islands that there was another side to him, too; that he was amazingly kind and giving, soft and well-spoken. We were colleagues at an event hosted by the Ritz-Carlton, at which well-known chefs—in addition to Tony and me that year, Daniel Boulud and Rick Bayless were in attendance—performed cooking demonstrations for high-paying guests.

Tony Bourdain was the heart of the weekend, an example of how good cooking should never be separated from a good heart. He was about people, and humanity, and the darkness that he had within himself was something he tried to keep away when he was giving to others. I was very saddened by his death in 2018. I'm not a depressive person, but I have empathy for him.

Kitchen culture has a long way to go. People need to be kinder. There need to be more women and more minorities in the kitchen. And young people who want to become chefs need to understand that the metric for success isn't the Michelin star. To me, the ultimate goal is to be inspired by one's interests and in turn to inspire others. Success is finding out who you really are and anchoring that discovery to a purpose. Cooking is a great love of my life, of course, but I still think of it as only a vehicle to show others that, by pursuing the thing we love in the face of life's obstacles, we truly find an end in itself.

Sixteen

———

MAMAN

A year or so after the opening of Atelier Crenn, Katherine turned to me one evening and said something shocking. "I helped you realize your dream," she said. "Now you have to help me realize mine." The restaurant, after a shaky start, was beginning to find its feet, and although Juan and I were still a few years away from being able to buy out the investors and set up the Crenn Dining Group—which we would own outright—business was starting to settle down. Katherine had stood by me throughout this period.

But having children wasn't something I had given much thought to. I loved my brother's kids, but having my own was never particularly a goal. I had always been focused on other things. Apart from Katherine and my close friends, my family in San Francisco was a rescue dog called Pascal—a Staffordshire terrier—who would later be joined by a Chihuahua called Maximus (who looks like a little rabbit and is my true baby). If Katherine had a baby, she and I were both clear we wouldn't share parental responsibility; the baby would be hers alone. But I wanted to help her as she had helped me, and intuitively I understood the strength of her need. We knew it might be a bumpy ride, both for her as a woman trying to get pregnant and for us in the context of our relationship.

The particulars of Katherine's journey to motherhood are not mine to tell, although I can say that it was amazing and I hope the small role I played was helpful. When things got hard, I pushed her. When she became discouraged, I refused to accept it. My bluntness, I know, can occasionally alienate, but it seemed to me the stakes were too high not to fight. After a few failed attempts at IVF and a lot of very difficult decision-making, I said, "Do you want a kid?"

"Yes," she said. "But we have to accept reality. Maybe this isn't meant to be." This is not, as you know, how I think.

"It's not a question of whether you're going to have kids," I said, "but of *how* you're going to have kids. We just have to find a way around this."

And we did. She did. My approach can be undiplomatic, but it comes from a place of love. There was something else, too; an open-mindedness about where one's children might come from that drills down into my deepest sense of self.

In 2014, two perfect babies were born. After four years together, Katherine and I were no longer a couple, but I was
still in the delivery room when they arrived. They came out
silver, shining like moonlight, and I cut the cord. It was beyond
words; amazing, beautiful, and I was honored to be there. I am
not their primary parent, nor officially their parent at all, but I
am present in their lives and I love them. It is as simple as that.
It was a busy year. In addition to the birth of Katherine's babies,
I geared up to open Petit Crenn, a smaller, more informal sister
restaurant to Atelier Crenn, in the Hayes Valley neighborhood
of the city.

If Atelier Crenn was a tribute to my father, then Petit Crenn
was devised with maman and my grandmother in mind. I
wanted it to mimic the vibe of a casual French bistro, the kind
of place where one might drop in and idle over lunch. The
menu is seafood heavy, although on any given day we might
offer a buckwheat crepe with escargot or a roast beet salad with
green onion, and the classic French brunch menu comes with
some upgrades.

When you order the Petit Crenn omelette, for example,
there is the option of white sturgeon caviar on the side. The
eggs Benedict is accompanied by smoked trout and braised
leeks. The dining room is bright and white and modern, with
the kind of warmth that can only come from an open kitchen

Maman and I in Paris.

and the ambience and smell of a wood-fired grill. My desire was to create a place that acted as an invitation to come and sit casually over a glass of wine, and to talk, always to talk.

If there is a real mission behind every business I run, it is this opportunity for human connection; the idea, going back to my adoption, that we are who we are based on the connections we make. As the Atelier took off, it was the success of this, of everything, that gave me the most pleasure. I think we are the only restaurant in history to have taken tables *out* after receiving a Michelin star, which we did in 2013. But all I ever wanted was to deepen the connection between the people in the kitchen and

The exterior of Petit Crenn on Hayes Street, San Francisco.

the people in the dining room, and once the menu had been perfected, scale was the only way to do it.

In March 2018, three years after opening Petit Crenn, I took over the venue next door to the Atelier and opened Bar Crenn, which I modeled after the Paris salons of the 1920s and '30s. I have always loved that era, between the two World Wars when, in France, people attended the public salons to eat and talk. I love everything about it—the style, the music, the whole of the art deco movement—but above all, the conversations, out of which so many artists, writers, and thinkers emerged. That is what I wanted to re-create.

The life of a chef can be nomadic. When you achieve prominence, you can travel all the time if you have a mind to, spending your life at cooking exhibitions in glamorous hotels or food conferences in luxury resorts. In my experience, enjoyable as these junkets can be, as you get older the attraction starts to wane. A little goes a long way. You have your expenses paid, but a lot of the time there is no fee. Without realizing it, you are giving your time away for free, and you need to be mindful of what you get out of these events. In 2014, I started to pivot more toward the kind of local events at which I could actually meet people with whom I share a community. It was at one of these that I met Nicole, who I would eventually marry.

When we first got together, Nicole lived in LA, an arrangement that may seem unideal to some, but I've always believed that a couple's ability to be apart can be a mark of true closeness, and even after she moved to San Francisco, we maintained separate apartments. The importance of being alone is one I have come to value more the older I've grown, and one that I connect to the pace of the restaurant. When I get home at night and on my rare days off, I long for quiet, while every morning, before heading into work, I take a moment to go out onto the terrace and watch the rowers doing their early-morning drills.

My house is my haven—a small, quiet, simple place, heavily inspired by my mother's straightforward good taste, with a fireplace and a lot of art on the walls. There is a painting of David Bowie, who I love, and a painting a friend did for me inspired by Jean Cocteau's 1929 novel, *Les Enfants Terribles*, one of my favorite books and movies of all time. Around the house are lots of images of dominos, as well as domino pieces I have collected from around the world. Domino was the nickname my father called me.

Seventeen

LA BELLE FRANCE

The question of family is one that will never stop intriguing me, the myriad pathways we take to one another. As I get older, my relationship with my own history changes. For a long time, I had very little curiosity about the woman who gave birth to me and who I was sure I could find if I tried. I even had a lead: the social workers kept track of my birth mother for over ten years after my adoption and they recorded that, many years after my adoption, she married. I have her husband's name, which would not be hard to trace. I would think about it occasionally, or a friend would encourage me to take a look. But I never did.

There were good reasons to hold back. There is a fear of what I might find. There is the fear of rejection, even after all these years. I have a lot of self-confidence, but there is a part of me that is still vulnerable and I can be quite insecure. The fear of finding my birth mother was partly a fear of retrospectively altering my own story by introducing new and unassailable elements, of having to adjust myself in order to accommodate her.

Also, I didn't need to. I don't mean this in a plaintive or flippant way. I mean it in the most positive way there is. My whole life I had thrilled with the possibilities opened up by the gaps in my history, and by the sense of movement and opportunity they gave me. It had been a big part of my drive. Why give that up? Why compromise something I had worked hard to perceive as a gift and replace it with something that might turn out to be limiting? I didn't need this information to complete my own story. I would complete it myself.

My brother did let me talk him into doing a DNA test recently, as I had done myself a few years earlier. DNA is a way for us to find out more about our origins without the potential disruption of tracing actual people—all the fun and none of the cost. Even my mother, for whom the whole question of our origins can be painful and difficult, got excited about the data my brother and I turned up.

Jean-Christophe is dark, like me, and we always assumed he had something like Iranian in his background. In fact, as it transpires, he is all European—French, English, Iberian, but nothing further afield than that—and nothing, it turns out, like me. As gene-reading technology improves, my DNA report changes slightly every few months to include new trace elements from Southeast Asia and Siberia. But it is still the case that I am predominantly North African—33 percent at the last count—and the rest primarily German and French.

Of these percentages, French represents the smallest proportion, just 7 percent of my DNA. And yet the older I get, the more French I feel. Although I left France in my early twenties, never to live there again, my thoughts and dreams still come to me in French. My most vivid memories, the foundation that feeds me, all originate in France. Even my priorities feel French—this in spite of the fact that when I lived in France, all I did was dream of going to America. Somehow these facts coexist. Part of my Frenchness feels like an absolute draw toward the beauty of things; the beauty of an object, food, a drawing, a poem—an inclination I have always at some level thought of as French. And of course I am aware of the central irony of my life: that one of the reasons I love France as much as I do is because I was able to leave.

The Élysée is the official residence of the president of France, a grand eighteenth-century building in the center of Paris that once belonged to Napoleon. I had walked past it as a college student a million times. Now I was back in Paris and about to walk in and make lunch.

It was 2017 and I had been invited to cook for Emmanuel Macron, the president of France, and a selection of the best chefs in the country. I have cooked for important people before, but this was different. I thought of how happy and proud my dad's old friend Albert Coquil would have been, and how proud it would have made my dad. The lunch had been organized by President Macron and his wife, Brigitte, to celebrate the best chefs in France and to award the trophy for the Bocuse d'Or, a biennial culinary championship held in Lyon and one of the most prestigious cooking competitions in the world.

The lunch itself was for three hundred people, drawn mainly from the French culinary world, and for the menu the organizers wanted to showcase five chefs, with a balance between women and men. I was chosen along with Guy Savoy, Anne-Sophie Pic, Yannick Alléno, and the pastry chef from Ladurée, Claire Heitzler. Each of us got to do a single dish.

This would be the very definition of a tough crowd, the realization of every stress dream from my youth in which the French culinary establishment had been gathered in one place to judge me. Alain Ducasse would be present, as would Joël Robuchon, Marc Veyrat, Philippe Etchebest, and Christian Constant, a roll call of the most famous French chefs in the world, plus, of course, the president of the Republic. When I flew to Paris that November, I was shaking at the prospect of what lay ahead. If I messed this up I would never recover.

When I arrived in the city, I went for a walk to calm down. I let my mind wander way back to my college boyfriend, Philippe, and to my mother's dinner parties at the house in Meudon. I bought some clothes for Katherine's girls—some gorgeous summer outfits. (She was annoyed; it was November and they wouldn't be able to wear them for months. This is the kind of thing I am always doing.) Finally, I headed over to the venue to meet my fate.

We were to serve lunch in the Salles des Fêtes, the grand reception room and a space of huge chandeliers, red drapes, and gilt wallpaper. I had thought very carefully about my dish. The safe thing, I knew, would be to stick to classic French cuisine, something purely in the tradition of the gastronomy we were celebrating. Then again, when have I ever played things safe?

Anne-Sophie Pic, the legendary chef who runs Maison Pic in Valence, in southwest France, did an exceptional oyster dish with black cardamom. Guy Savoy—the celebrated, multi-Michelin-starred chef who owns five restaurants in Paris—did a beautiful artichoke soup with black truffle and a brioche puff stuffed with mushrooms. In the end, I did a dish that took from traditional French cooking and combined it with my other culinary interests: Japanese rice, pickled seaweed, and broth with langoustines, with fermented pineapple on the side. It was light, fresh, with a beautiful layering of flavor. It was very French, no question. But it had its roots in other things.

After the event, we were all highly praised and thanked by the president. But it wasn't until Alain Ducasse—one of the most celebrated French chefs of the modern era whose restaurants have collectively won over twenty-one Michelin stars—came over and told me my food was exceptional that I realized just how nervous I'd been. I hadn't trained with these people. I hadn't earned my spurs in a French kitchen or slogged through

A very French occasion.

the brutal internship of a French cooking school. I had skipped all that, and although I had spent my entire career telling myself it was no big deal and that I'd made the right choice, at some level, I realized, I had been seeking the approval of the world I left behind. Over thirty years after leaving France, I felt as if I finally had the nod of my peers.

Eighteen months later, I was honored with the Ordre National du Mérite, one of the greatest awards the French government can give. The ceremony was presided over by Emmanuel

Contemplating knighthood in front of my flag.

Lebrun-Damiens, the consul general of France in San Francisco, who before he handed me the blue-and-silver medal said, "With this award, France recognizes in Dominique Crenn a chef, an artist, and an activist. Her cooking draws inspiration from French cuisine while reinventing classic French food. An experience in her restaurants is an all-embracing artwork, as in music or architecture. And through her gastronomy, she gets involved with the city and the world, in a willingness to address the challenges facing our time."

I couldn't have asked for a better summary of my work, nor hoped for more meaningful recognition. I was feeling on top of the world. The Atelier had received its third Michelin star in November, and Bar Crenn, which had been open for less than twelve months, had received its first star. *Paris Match* did a spread. *Rolling Stone* came. By January, it was clear that 2019 was shaping up to be our best year yet in the restaurant and my diary was booked solid through December.

On top of all this, there were two beautiful four-year-olds in my life, a wife I adored, and a kitchen full of people who were as close to me as family. In the rare moments I had to take stock, it occurred to me that the life I had created for myself was entirely on my own terms. I thought back to those days of my childhood when, looking down through my window at the orphanage in Meudon, I had wondered how much further I might travel. It was something that, in the coming months, I would have greater cause to think about than ever before.

Eighteen

—————

NEW BEGINNINGS

I t was the week of my fifty-fourth birthday and Nicole and I were in Brooklyn. This was a rare trip for us in that it was entirely without work pretext. No tour of the hotel kitchens, no cooking exhibitions in the evening or mandatory appearance at a party sponsored by a leading champagne brand. Simply a break to celebrate my birthday and spend time with each other. We had already been up to Blue Hill at Stone Barns, Dan Barber's phenomenal restaurant in upstate New York, and were due to visit a few art galleries. We were having a wonderful time.

The day before my birthday, we returned to the city to hang out and wind down. It was that evening, in the hotel room, that we found a lump in my right breast. I was alarmed, of course. But I wasn't unduly panicked. I've always been healthy, and at that point had never even had a mammogram. When I rang my doctor in San Francisco, however, she spoke without hesitation. Come back immediately, she said.

The previous few months had been intense. My schedule, already overloaded, had snowballed since the Atelier had gained its third Michelin star. In early spring, I had cooked at a gala dinner in LA alongside Suzanne Tracht and Nancy Silverton, and served as a judge at the S.Pellegrino Young Chef award. In June, I was due to go to Singapore to pick up an award. The Atelier had landed at number 35 on The World's 50 Best Restaurants list, an upgrade from the previous year when I'd complained about being relegated to in the Best Female Chef category. Prior to that evening in Brooklyn, my main source of irritation had been that the organizers for this award had still asked me to sit on an all-woman panel. (I'd refused.)

Now all of that faded into the background. As Nicole and I flew back to San Francisco from New York, I rationalized that I had little to worry about. I lead a pretty healthy lifestyle. I eat well, I don't drink too much, I don't smoke, and I had just cut out coffee. I don't go to the gym, but I am on my feet running around all day. The life of a chef is very strenuous. Apart from the months when I was recovering from my accident, I had always felt physically strong. And the fact was I didn't have time to be ill. The next day, after visiting the doctor and having the mammogram, I couldn't imagine this would be anything but a horrible false alarm.

One of the obvious downsides to the blank slate of my adoption is that I have no medical history for either of my biological parents. If there is a predisposition in my genes toward certain conditions, I will never know it. A few days later, when the results of the mammogram came in, they dropped out of a completely blue sky. Although they were inconclusive, the results of the scan described a state of precancer—that is, the doctor explained, stage-0 breast cancer that would require treatment. This was the best possible diagnosis short of an all-clear, but even hearing the word "precancer" plunged me into despair. I needed to go in for a biopsy, which a few days later I did. And then I waited.

At the best of times, I am not good at waiting. Those few days were impossibly hard. For the first time in a long time, I felt myself start to panic. I thought of my father at the end of his life. He became extremely lethargic during treatment, and although he was upbeat and brave, I realized that after watching him suffer I had become very frightened of cancer.

I let my mind race ahead through various scenarios. The restaurant was on a roll and had never been more successful— we had even bought a Molteni for the kitchen, the fifty-thousand-dollar handmade Italian stove of my dreams. I was fielding more offers for cooking events and appearances than I could possibly hope to accept. And I was working on plans for Boutique Crenn, a $7-million boulangerie-patisserie set to open the following year, in San Francisco's Salesforce Tower. In the event that the results of the biopsy were bad, I would have to radically reprioritize. I didn't want to pull back from the day-to-day of managing a team I loved, but I also had to re-center. What did I want to do with the next five years of my life? Where exactly should I be directing my efforts?

I was reminded that my life as a chef was never just about food, not even way back at the beginning. If someone wants to talk to me about food, I immediately want to expand the conversation outward to discover their view on poverty, or East versus West, or the environment—anything that might broaden my insight into the way they think. The possibility of being sick only deepened this desire to use every moment of my life to make connections with others.

A few days later, the results of the biopsy came in. The doctor told me they were worse than the mammogram had implied. I did not, in fact, have stage-0 breast cancer, but a more invasive cancer in the tissue that the scan had failed to pick up. The doctor described it as "triple-negative" breast cancer, which had advanced to stage 2.

Triple negative, I have since learned, is a tricky cancer to treat to the extent that the cancer cells test negative for hormone receptors such as estrogen and progesterone, which inhibits the treatment options. On the plus side, it is a form of breast cancer that is known to respond well to chemotherapy. I would need three months of weekly chemo sessions, said the doctor, and surgery after that. The good news was that the cancer hadn't spread and I tried to focus on this. But the words "good news" simply didn't compute in the context of what I'd been told. It was a huge shock that I couldn't immediately absorb.

I tend to trust my instincts, even when they run against the advice everyone else is giving me. In the days after the diagnosis, I felt mired in sadness and disbelief, but also convinced with every fiber of my being that the only way to get through the next few months was to look outward, not to shut myself in.

Without hesitation, I told my friends and my team at the restaurant I had been diagnosed with breast cancer. Within a week, I had posted news of my diagnosis on Instagram. For a few days, I lost myself in the distraction of canceling everything—the trip to Singapore, trips to France and Canada after that—clearing my schedule right up to the fall.

And then I sat down and tried to think about how I would handle this. Within hours of posting on Instagram, I had received an overwhelming volume of messages of support, from chefs across the industry as well as scores of people who had been through what I was about to experience. The effect was like a boost to my immune system.

I started to bring myself back up. Okay, I said, here's a new challenge. And what does that mean? If there's anything I know how to do in this life it is to find opportunity in a bleak situation, to take bad news and turn it into an invitation for rebirth. That is how I am trying to deal with this. My cancer diagnosis is horrific and unwanted, but it might yet help me to make the best of my life. I don't know how I will feel at the end of my treatment, or how this might change the course of my next twenty years, but I know one indisputable fact: I'm a warrior!

To look in the mirror has never been an uncomplicated act for me. I never saw my maman or dad. I saw myself in isolation, a dreamer and also someone who struggles. I saw my weakness and my strength—my weakness being a case of feeling too much, my strength a determination to turn that feeling into action. A few weeks into chemotherapy, I look in the mirror and see something else again. The physical reality of someone undergoing cancer treatment is less horrifying to me than it might have been, perhaps, to someone who had always taken their own image for granted.

On my first day of chemo, a friend wrote a poem for me. She called it "Dear Chemo" and I posted it on Instagram. It was an unusual approach, I know, to address the treatment directly, and not only address it, but to praise it. I had a hunch that falling into the habit of hating and resenting my treatment would only make enduring it worse. The bottom line was, it was saving me. Cancer treatment has come a long way since my father died, and the only possible response, it seemed to me, was to shout to the heavens with gratitude. "Dear Chemo," the poem read, "Oh how I thank you / Thank you for your healing / Thank you for lighting up the dark spaces / Thank you thank you a million times thank you."

I wanted to normalize my illness as much as possible and try to accept it as a part of my life. I wanted to put my cancer in a category that didn't alienate me from my physical self. Cancer affects millions of people every year, but there is still a tendency to look at it as removed from us, as something terrifying that falls outside of all human systems and that we struggle to talk about and share. I didn't want that. I wanted to be able to absorb it as a frightening but faceable part of life's journey.

And I wanted to wring out of it every shred of closeness it gave me to other people. A diagnosis like this allows you to look inside yourself. It's kind of beautiful. It makes you think about what is important and how you want to live your life. Was I focused too much on being successful—always pushing myself to the next stage—at the expense of concentrating on what I needed as a human being? How did I want the next stage of my life to look?

Perhaps it was inevitable that one result of all this thinking was that Nicole and I would split up. It wasn't acrimonious and she is still steadfastly a part of my family, continuing to come with me on visits to the hospital. But after some years of soul-searching, we came to the realization that we would be better off as friends. She is the best kind of person, someone who I know will always show up for me, and yet we are both curious enough to want to move on. With love, we decided to let each other go.

I am not a big crier. A cartoon can make me cry, or seeing an animal suffer, but I tend not to cry for myself. It's not my style and it's not how I deal with things. But those first days of treatment were tough. The chemo itself wasn't painful, although the feeling of having chemicals flow through my body

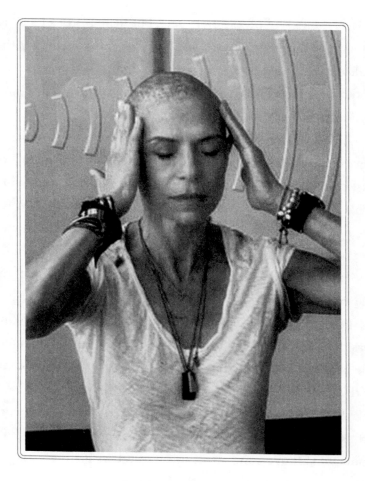

was unnerving. What disturbed me more was how wiped out I felt afterward. It made my usual approach to unhappiness—action—impossible, and for a few days I lay around in my apartment in a state of exhaustion and shock.

For my second session, the doctors put in a port above my chest. This way, they said, they wouldn't have to find a new vein every time. It wasn't painful, but again I felt wiped out afterward. I started to make mental adjustments, to understand that I can be a warrior but that it's also okay to be weak. I had to set limits for myself, so that during the months of treatment I still had usable energy and I was taking self-care seriously, signing up for ancillary therapies like acupuncture and focusing on feeling excited to get rid of the cancer. I reminded myself daily that you can't be afraid of change, even when that change seems bad.

Two weeks into my chemotherapy, my entire staff at the Atelier gathered in one of the restaurant's back rooms. One by one they sat down, grinning, and offered their heads to the hairdresser standing behind them. One by one she shaved off their hair with an electric razor. It was one of the most amazing experiences of my life, full of laughter and solidarity and unity. Now we all have shaved heads, a sense of the ridiculousness of life, and the giddiness of going through it together. How can I resent this experience when, for all the terror and pain, it has opened a door to a deeper connection with the people around me? I have never felt so loved.

It made me think about my birth mother—how she had tried and failed to keep me. How unloved she must have felt as a child and later on. For years, she was buffeted about with no anchor, and while I had always felt sympathy toward her, now I felt something else. For the first time, I found myself wanting to find her. I called the French consulate in San Francisco and they said they would help.

If the call comes through and she's still in France, I'll fly to meet her. It's not about finding out who I am at this stage and it's not even about curiosity. It's about doing what I do best— moving on. Getting sick feels like the beginning of a new chapter, and in seeking my birth mother, I'm ready, finally, to turn the page on the old.

My journey with cancer also led to something truly unexpected and wonderful. I fell in love. There were countless people who wished me well and helped me get through one of the most difficult times in my life, and I am forever grateful to them. But I also fell in love with Maria, a friend I had met a year before and with whom formed an unbelievable connection, without which I am not sure I would have managed to remain so positive. Following a double mastectomy and a good diagnosis late in 2019, I went to Paris with Maria and proposed to her. Like Juan says, I pull the trigger. I knew that I loved Maria deeply and I didn't want to waste any time.

Before my diagnosis, we had been discussing alterations to the menu at the Atelier to accommodate the change in the season. I had gone up to the farm to see how the crops were progressing. As climate change takes hold, each season lasts longer and vegetables come in earlier than they used to. I thought about this as I wandered around. I thought about native American plants, and wondered if I could find examples that nobody uses in cooking and that have a strong story behind them. As so often happens when I go up to Sonoma, I thought about my grandmother's farm.

The farm in spring is a beautiful place, a forecast of the future and a memory all in one. I walked around, inspecting the crops and saying hi to the hens, while the sun shone warm on my back. It was my grandmother who taught me that what you put into the soil you take out again, and that the soil and the sea are where life begins. For a moment, I visualized the potato field in Brittany, the men pausing to wipe their brows in the summer heat before digging back down into the heap of potatoes. There are times when the smell of sun, sweat, and earth is everything there is.

Up at the farm in Sonoma, the cauliflower was ripening. There was a lot of green garlic coming up. It was way too early in the season, but we even had peas. I crouched down for a moment and took a tendril in hand. How many hundreds of times had I done this before? Picked a vegetable and brushed the soil from its roots? And yet it never ceases to amaze me. There it was, the tiny green shoot, hopeful, vibrant, unbelievably strong, pushing its way up through the earth toward sunlight.

Conclusion

HOMECOMING

When I look back on my twenty-four-year-old self, I am astonished by how little I knew. Thirty years ago, when I left France, I was a young woman heading into the unknown, buoyed by a single certainty: that change requires action and action requires movement. I wanted my life to change. I made the necessary movement. I could only hope things would work out.

Everything did change, in some ways. I learned a new language and a new way of living. I found a way through the world that, in my youth, I had no idea even existed. Those half-formed dreams I had in my teens and early twenties materialized in ways I couldn't have possibly imagined.

When I look back, however, it's less in the spirit of measuring how far I've come than of marveling at how much was there from the beginning. I sometimes envisage my life as a fiddlehead fern, the future tucked tightly inside itself, with everything I would become already in there, waiting.

I couldn't always see it. So much of my life has been guided by instinct that occasionally, when my instincts have veered too far from the norm, I've lost my nerve and made bad decisions. I have followed the crowd. I have acted from a place of insecurity and panic, and that is always when things have gone wrong. Each time, I have found my way home by reminding myself of the irrefutable things that I know.

I know that there is always another way. I know that the reward of doing things differently is worth the anxiety of not fitting in. I know that inside every seemingly bad situation a new opportunity is waiting. I know not to sign a contract without reading the small print and I know that you need good lawyers if you're going into business. If you really think you can do something, I know that more often than not you can. These are things I used to know at an instinctual level; now, through experience, I know them for sure.

I have a million ideas for the future. Some of them will work, some won't. The only way to find out is by doing them, and if what happens next is uncertain, I thrill to the possibility of change. On the worst days, I try to remain curious and to hang on to my courage. And I come back to this, every time: Life is about togetherness. I know this as well as I know myself. It's the most powerful thing that we have.

Acknowledgments

To Ann Godoff,
thank you for your trust, and for letting me
tell the world my story.

To Casey Denis
and the rest of the Penguin Press team, thank you.

To Michael Psaltis,
my agent, thank you.

To Mika Takeuchi,
thank you for showing up.

To Laura Carrillo,
a true friend that has always been there for me
no matter what, we will never stop laughing.

To Katherine Keon,
you inspire me. Thank you for being in my life and
sharing the gift of life, Charlotte and Olivia.

ACKNOWLEDGMENTS

To Lucky Rapp,
you are extraordinary. Thank you for your
unconditional love and friendship.

To Laurent DuPont,
merci pour ta grande amitié, jet'aime.

To Kristen Hetland,
thank you for being you and lifting me up
anytime I needed it. Most of all, thank
you for loving me.

To Tiffany Bushnell,
thank you for your wicked mind and
your amazing friendship.

To Nicole Mackinlay Hahn and Jill Andresevic,
you have given me so much through the years,
I am honored to be your friend and to be on this
creative journey with both of you.

To Russell Jackson,
I love you, my friend.

To Maria Canabal,
You have showed me what friendship is about,
and unconditional love. Thank you.

To all my friends, my team, and my business
partner, thank you for believing in me.